CLASSIC CARS

THE GOLDEN YEARS

CLASSIC CARS

THE GOLDEN YEARS

Martin Buckley

HERMES HOUSE

For Catherine and Sean

This edition published by Hermes House
an imprint of
Anness Publishing Limited
Hermes House
88-89 Blackfriars Road
London SE1 8HA

A CIP catalogue record for this book is available from the British Library

ISBN 1 84038 151 5

Publisher: Joanna Lorenz
Editor: Joanne Rippin
Assistant Editor: Emma Gray
Designer: Alan Marshall

Previously published as part of a larger compendium, *The Encyclopedia of Classic Cars*

Printed and bound in Singapore

© Anness Publishing Limited 1998
Updated © 1999
1 3 5 7 9 10 8 6 4 2

The publishers would like to thank *Classic and Sportscar* magazine, Haymarket Specialist
Motoring, for supplying most of the pictures in the book. Additional pictures supplied by:
BFI Stills, Posters and Designs: pp 58mt, 59tl/mb.
Don Morley: p 54. John Colley: p 1, 14m.
National Motor Museum, Beaulieu, England: pp 3 (N Wright), 44.
b=bottom, t=top, l=left, r=right, m=middle.

CONTENTS

INTRODUCTION

As government regulations threaten to engineer much of the character out of modern cars, as our roads become more congested and dangerous and the air we breathe gets more contaminated, we can look back to the "classic" era of the 1950s and 1960s as the romantic Golden Age of the motorcar. In Europe, more and better mass-produced cars were seen as a liberating force for families previously restricted to public transport. In North America, cars simply got bigger, reflecting the wealth and confidence of the most powerful nation on earth. Traffic was yet to reach its often gridlocked state of today, petrol was much cheaper and, in Britain at least, there were no speed restrictions on the newly-opened motorways.

Before the mergers and close-downs of the 1970s, buyers could choose from a far wider range of makes reflecting national identities. The Japanese motor industry, later so dominant, was not even a speck on the horizon in the 1950s and 1960s. In engineering and styling, too, cars tended to be more varied and individual – you could tell an Austin from a Morris, a Vauxhall from a Volvo without having to look at the badge. Safety was optional: it was speed, glamour and style that sold cars, and in the 50s and early 60s nobody had even begun to think of the exhaust-emission regulations that would strangle power outputs in the 70s. Back then, the motorcar was our servant. Now, through its very proliferation, it has become our master. In this book, we celebrate the glory days and beyond and the marvellous machines which rode through them, fixing in our cultural consciousness a picture of the ideal motor – the classic car.

The Classic Era

Today we're hooked on nostalgia. As hopeless escapists, nothing feeds our need
better than an old car - a classic car. After the Second World War, the motorcar came
of age. As more and more people around the world took to the road, manufacturers
began to stretch the boundaries. The makers set styling, engineering and safety trends
in an increasingly competitive market: speeds increased; styling and engineering
became more adventurous; many devices we take for granted today, like disc brakes,
four-wheel drive (4-WD) and automatic transmission, became widely used. The
1950s, 1960s and to an extent the 1970s were the most fertile period for the motorcar,
a classic era and a perfect breeding ground for the classic car we cherish today, be it
limousine or economy runabout, sportscar or apparently humdrum saloon.

EVOLUTION OF THE MOVEMENT

As the 20th century draws to a close, we seem to look back as much as forward, pining for what were, as we see it, better times. We can't revisit our Golden Age, but at least we can own and experience the material objects that evoke it: clothes, music, films and cars – classic cars. Glamorous, kitsch, humble or high bred, these mobile time warps powerfully conjure up a particular period.

New Vintage

The hobby of preserving and collecting cars built after the Second World War began to take shape in the early 1970s. Veteran (pre-1905), Edwardian (pre-1919) and Vintage (pre-1931) cars – as defined by Britain's Vintage Sports Car Club – have always been easy enough to categorize but, by the end of the 1960s, post-war motorcars of the better kind were coming of age. To call them simply "old cars" no longer seemed appropriate: whether beautiful, fast or technically pre-eminent, the post-1945 car had at its best all the gravitas of the pre-war machinery. Slowly, quietly, the "new Vintage" had arrived, filling the gap between Vintage and

■ ABOVE *Classics so evocative of their period as these – the AC Ace, Ferrari 166 and C-Type Jaguar – have always been in strong demand and are priced at a premium.*

■ BELOW *Racing cars with some historic significance are eagerly sought by collectors and achieve astonishing prices at auction.*

modern for a new generation of enthusiasts.

One-marque clubs for well-bred sporting marques such as Aston and Bentley had been around for years, but as enthusiasts for the less exalted makes felt the need to huddle together around a common banner, many new guilds and registers sprouted. Traditionalists had long complained that modern cars all "looked the same", but in the 70s there was a gut feeling that the motorcar had seen its best years as safety and pollution regulations made inroads into designers' freedom. Styling, particularly in Britain, seemed to be losing its way.

No wonder older cars began to look increasingly attractive. They were plentiful, cheap, easy to work on and still very usable on increasingly busy roads. Drive an old car and you made a statement about your individualism: you weren't prepared to become just another faceless, sterile tin can on the bypass to oblivion or obsessed with keeping up with the Joneses in the yearly new-model scrum. It all came together in 1973 when a UK magazine, *Classic Cars*, was launched.

The name "classic" stuck, a useful catch-all term for a sprawling, ill-defined genre that in

■ ABOVE *High prices obtained by auction houses for high-grade classics had a knock-on effect on the rest of the industry.*

■ BELOW *Classic-car dealers prospered in the late 1980s as prices went out of control.*

just 20 years or so has blossomed from an eccentric pastime in to a multimillion-pound industry. Not much happened for about ten years, until about 1982-83 when the nature of the hobby began to change dramatically. Slowly, under the noses of true enthusiasts, market forces took hold as it dawned on investors that really prime machinery could prove a fine hedge against inflation or an appreciating asset. Suddenly, the market hardened as Americans came to Europe seeking prime collectables.

At first, gilt-edged pre-war hardware – Bentley, Bugatti, etc. – set the pace in auction rooms but, by mid-decade, supercars of the 50s, 60s and 70s were hyped on their coat tails. Once affordable Ferraris, Astons and Jaguar XKs and E-Types became "investor" cars,

commodities too expensive and precious to be driven (which was rather missing the point).

As the auction houses pulled even bigger numbers, hype went into overdrive. Banks and finance companies offered loans to buy classics. The increasing ranks of classic-car magazines bulged with advertizing. Enthusiasts' gentle hobby was turned into an ugly brawl driven by greed. Many found themselves with cars that were worth more than their houses, machinery they were now too nervous to use. The boom couldn't last, fortunately. The recession hit in 1989 and demand quickly fell.

A hobby again

Today, the investors are long gone, the market is stable and the cars are where they should be – with enthusiasts. Though we are unlikely to see such madness again, rare and high-calibre thoroughbred cars – especially those with a racing pedigree or an interesting provenance – will always be in strong demand. Fashion still has its part to play in the lower echelons of the market, but those who bought Citroëns and Jaguars have learnt about the dedication required to run an old car. Some went back to their moderns, others caught a lifelong bug.

TECHNICAL DEVELOPMENTS

In the beginning, cars were motorized horse carriages or, in the case of the three-wheeled Benz of 1889, relied heavily on cycle technology. Most cars were braked only by the rear wheel; steering, often by tiller, was slow and ponderous. A shoulder-high centre of gravity threatened to tip the car over. All this was containable at the 4mph (6.4kph) first allowed in Britain for motor vehicles and not too scary at the 14mph (22.5kph) allowed by 1896, but as speeds rose, something had to be done. Makers who introduced each refinement created classics along the way.

Technology filters down

Excellence began with high-class cars such as the Rolls-Royce and Bentley. Steadily, the technology filtered down to such humble transport as the Austin Seven. By the start of

■ LEFT *Cord's 810 used a supercharged V-eight Lycoming engine with revolutionary front-wheel drive.*

■ BELOW *The Chrysler Airflow was one of the first cars designed with an eye to aerodynamics.*

■ LEFT AND BELOW *The Lancia Aprillia was a groundbreaking saloon of the mid-1930s.*

the Second World War, bodies were generally made of steel, sat on a separate chassis, and there were brakes all round. Jaguar brought disc brakes to the world's notice at Le Mans in 1953; five years later they appeared on Jaguar's road cars and soon every maker used them.

Refinement follows

Four-wheel drive, with antilock brakes, was pioneered by Ferguson Formula. It first appeared in a passenger car on the Jensen FF of 1966, along with Dunlop Maxaret anti-lock brakes derived from aircraft technology. It was expensive and complex – only 320 were built.

Overhead camshafts allow more direct

operation of valves and a better combustion-chamber shape. They were used on specialist racing cars such as the Alfa Romeo and Bugatti from the 20s onwards and were introduced to the mainstream in the straight-six XK engine in the 120 of 1948. Soon, makers realized they could run double overhead camshafts and multivalve layouts.

Self-levelling was a standard feature of the futuristic DS launched in 1955 by Citroën. Even the cheaper 2CV had a modicum of levelling, because front and rear suspension were interconnected by springs. The British Motor Corporation (BMC) 1100 and 1800 of the 60s – and Minis of the period – are interconnected hydraulically. Self-levelling was used at the tail end of the Range Rover from its launch in 1970.

Front-wheel drive, used by BSA, Cord and Citroën since the 30s, did not hit the mainstream until the Mini appeared in 1959. While scorned by purists, this layout makes for

■ ABOVE *A 1956 Chevy: crude - but comfortable and well equipped.*

■ RIGHT *The Citroën 2CV: quirky, uncomfortable and poorly equipped. So who cares!*

■ BELOW RIGHT *The revolutionary Mini, a masterpiece of packaging.*

■ BELOW *The boxy body design of Lancia's Flavia an expensively-engineered, superb-handling car.*

safe, predictable handling and better packaging – more interior room for a given size – than rear-driven counterparts.

All the while, chassis improvements and tyre technology shadowed each other: Citroën's *Traction-avant* was the first car to use radial tyres, the narrow and distinctively treaded Michelin X.

America thinks big

In America, spacious cars with powerful, six- and eight-cylinder engines were common, even before the war. Makers loaded cars with every device to take the work out of driving: automatic transmission, power steering, power brakes, air conditioning, self-dipping headlamps. Engines, generally understressed by large capacity, showcased maintenance-free features such as hydraulic tappets (initially used for quietness).

MILESTONE MODELS

The following are technically important cars that made history from the 1930s to the 1970s, and had a lasting impact on the industry.

Citroën *Traction Avant*

Front-wheel drive and monocoque construction – in 1934! All this and unrivalled ride and handling from low centre of gravity and all-independent-torsion bar suspension came from the fertile mind of André Citroën.

Fiat 500

Dante Giacosa's master-stroke, the Italian car for the masses, was the Topolino. It was a full-sized car scaled down, with a tiny four-cylinder engine but all-steel unitary construction and independent suspension. (John Cooper plundered this for rear-engined racers.)

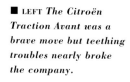

■ LEFT *The Citroën Traction Avant was a brave move but teething troubles nearly broke the company.*

■ BELOW *Spaceship: just imagine the effect of the Citroën DS's shape on the public in 1955.*

Citroën DS/SM

When launched to a stunned public in 1955, the DS looked like a spaceship. Its incredible other-worldly body style by Flaminio Bertoni used easily-removable outer panels; it had a glass-fibre roof and tail-lamps like rockets. A pressurised, self-levelling gas and oil system replaced suspension springs, and also pwered the brakes, steering, clutch and even gear change. Its complexity scared off many buyers.

■ BELOW *Fiat 500: poor man's transport, now the darling of the trendy.*

Mini

Alec Issigonis's revolutionary Mini of 1959 set the convention for every small car since and is a strong candidate for the most significant car of the 20th century. By mounting the engine transversely and making it drive the front wheels (not a first: Alvis, sundry American companies and Fiat had tried it before), Issigonis fitted space for four adults into a package 10ft (3m) long.

To keep the driveline package very short, the gearbox sat under the engine, in the sump. The use of a 10 in (25.5cm) wheel at each corner not only minimized the encroachment of

Jaguar E-type

With its gorgeous, curvy, phallic shape derived from Malcolm Sayers's Le Mans-winning D-Type racer, combined with a 3.8-litre version of the classic XK engine, this is the car that epitomized the racy end of the Swinging 60s. It was fantastic value at its 1961 launch price equivalent of only four Minis – and early versions really would come near the alleged top speed of 150mph (241kph). Forget the crunchy gearbox and unpredictable brakes, this is one of the world's most desirable cars.

Datsun 240Z

The Japanese had really arrived in 1969 with this "Big Healey" beater. Its classic fastback shape has never been bettered by Japan, and the strong, 2.4-litre straight-six engine made all the right noises. Good handling came from its all-independent strut suspension and super performance from its relatively light weight. Later cars – the 260 and 280Z – became heavier and softer. As is so often the case, first is purest. This is Japan's first classic and the world's best-selling sportscar.

wheel-arch space into the passenger compartment but, together with the direct rack-and-pinion steering and firm, rubber suspension, took handling to new standards of "chuckability". The Mini is still made to the same familiar specifications, although big changes are predicted for the model in the new millenium.

The Mini has competed since it first appeared; most notable performances were ace Paddy Hopkirk's wins in Alpine rallies in the 60s, his finest moment being victory in the 1965 Monte Carlo Rally. Minis still hold their own in historic rallying in the 90s.

■ ABOVE *The 246 Dino, one of the most gorgeous shapes ever, although it never badged Ferrari.*

■ RIGHT *Datsun's 240Z took on the mantle of the "Big Healey" - a lusty six banger for the 1970s.*

LEADING ENGINEERS

These are some of the most innovative and imaginative engineers from the world motor industry.

André Citroën

A true innovator, Citroën followed his own direction to produce cars that led the world for refinement and technical innovation. His engineeering tour de force, the *Traction-avant* of 1934, was followed up by his utilitarian masterstroke, the 2CV of 1948.

Ferdinand Porsche

Porsche designed the world's best-selling car, the VW Beetle which became the basis for the Porsche 356 designed by his son Ferry, forerunner of the immortal 911.

Alec Issigonis

Issigonis's masterstroke was the Mini, a brilliant piece of packaging whose layout – transverse engine, front-wheel drive and an

■ ABOVE *André Citroën carried a torch for innovation; much of the detailed design work was done by others.*

■ ABOVE RIGHT *Ferry Porsche, son of the man responsible for the world's best-selling car, himself made a vital contribution – the 356.*

■ LEFT *Alec Issigonis left his legacy in the shape of two brilliant small cars, the Morris Minor and the immortal Mini.*

independently-sprung wheel at each corner – has been copied for every other small car in the world. But people forget he was also reponsible for the Morris Minor, the best-handling and most modern car of its generation.

Antonio Fessia

Engineering supremo behind the classic Lancia Fulvia – and its bigger siblings the Flavia and Flaminia – Professor Antonio Fessia joined Fiat in 1925. By 1936, at only 35, he was director of the central technical office. Under him, Dante Giacosa designed the Topolino. A demanding, sometimes difficult boss, Fessia approached design scientifically. His 1960 Lancia Flavia, harking back to the 47 Cemsa Caproni, was the first Italian car with front-wheel drive. He followed up with the smaller V-four Fulvia which shared many components. He stayed with Lancia until his death in 1968.

William Lyons

Lyons was responsible for the beautiful styling of his Jaguars, from SS through MkII to XJ6 –

all classics. Another achievement was to keep prices low without sacrificing quality – Lyons's Jaguars were always superb value. An autocratic boss, he started Swallow Sidecars in the mid-1920s, at first building sidecars, then fitting more luxurious bodywork to Austin Sevens. The first SS Jaguars, brilliantly styled saloons and a beautiful SS100 sportscar appeared in the mid-1930s, all-time styling greats from Lyon's fertile pen. After the Second World War, his company became Jaguar.

■ ABOVE LEFT *WO Bentley was a gifted engineer, but he soon left the company that bore his name and went to Lagonda.*

■ ABOVE RIGHT *Colin Chapman, a brilliant and innovative designer, produced some of the best-handling cars ever.*

■ LEFT *Sir William Lyons, a great designer and an intuitive stylist: his cars always looked like a million dollars but represented superb value for money.*

Colin Chapman

A truly gifted structural engineer whose radical designs changed the face of racing – the road-car operation was intended only to shore up the racing effort. His first self-built car and the legendary Lotus Seven hit the road in 1953 and 1957 respectively. Chapman's weight-paring efforts, all for agility and speed, sometimes earned criticism for risking driver safety. He was devastated by the death of his star driver and friend Jim Clark in 1968.

Dante Giacosa

Dante Giacosa studied mechanical engineering at Turin Polytechnic and joined Fiat in 1928. From 1933 he was involved in the design of a small car. He put his watercooled Topolino against an aircooled design and won. More than four million Topolino's were made, taking their rightful place as one of the world's great small cars beside the Austin 7, the VW Beetle and the Mini.

Giacosa then created most archetypal small Italian cars, including the Fiat Nuova 500, 600, 127 and 128, and the masterpieces 8V and Cisitalia racer. He died in 1996.

MASS PRODUCTION

Henry Ford started it all with his Model T Ford. Production began in America in 1908 and later began in Britain. By 1913, Ford's plant at Old Trafford, Manchester, was making 8,000 cars a year by mass production whilst traditionalist Wolseley could manage only 3,000.

Where English cars were largely produced by hand, with chassis parts being individually made, drilled, reamed and assembled, Ford invested in huge machine tools that would

■ BELOW LEFT AND RIGHT *Henry Ford's automated production lines speeded car making, here a row of Model T's, beyond belief. He took his new methods to England, setting up a factory in Old Trafford, Manchester. In 1913 it could make 8,000 cars a year.*

stamp out parts by the hundred, exactly the same every time, which did not need skilled labour to assemble.

The cost of these tools was huge, so selling the resulting cars cheaply in huge numbers was the answer. Where car bodies had traditionally been made by hand, all to slightly different specifications, Ford's T's were, with a few variations on the theme, all the same and had pressed and welded bodies, like today's cars. Spray painting saved hours over the traditional multicoat process with its laborious rubbing down by hand between coats.

■ LEFT *A test track was built on the roof of Fiat's factory at Lingotto, Turin.*

■ RIGHT *The Pininfarina factory hand-building bodies for the Ferrari 330 GT.*

Conveyor-belt cars

To achieve this huge production, Ford installed its first moving-track assembly operations in Detroit, Michigan, the world's largest car-manufacturing centre, and in Trafford Park, Manchester, England. Instead of men moving to the cars to complete their specialist operation, or pushing cars by hand from one assembly station to another, the cars came to the men for each additional operation to be completed, with components fed in from overhead conveyors. Each man would walk beside the chassis until his task was completed and repeat the exercise on the next chassis. By the end of the line, the car was complete. Ford's basic T two-seater, the runabout, was produced in 1913. A classic was born.

Gradually, all other makers followed, although luxury cars were still largely hand built, just as prestige classics always have been. Morgan still hand builds cars in the same way it has since the 1920s, rolling partially-completed cars from one station to another. Yet by 1927, Citroën was producing a car every 10 minutes.

■ ABOVE *Fiat 850 coupés on production lines at Turin.*

■ BELOW *Ford Anglias being sprayed on a moving line at Dagenham, Essex. In time, robots replaced people.*

Robots lend a hand

Even greater speed and productivity were achieved by the use of power tools, suspended from the ceiling so they could be manhandled more easily. The next step was to cut manpower. First, spray painting was robotized, then the welding of bodyshells. To show how production methods continue to progress, of cars made today the one needing the most labour-intensive welding on its bodyshell is the Mini, first seen in 1959.

It was through mass production that cars such as the MG were born. The first MG Midget of 1929 used simple components borrowed from the Morris saloon cars in a more sporty body, just as all MGs since have done, right up to the F of 1995. Thanks to mass production, classic sportscars were made available to the general buying public.

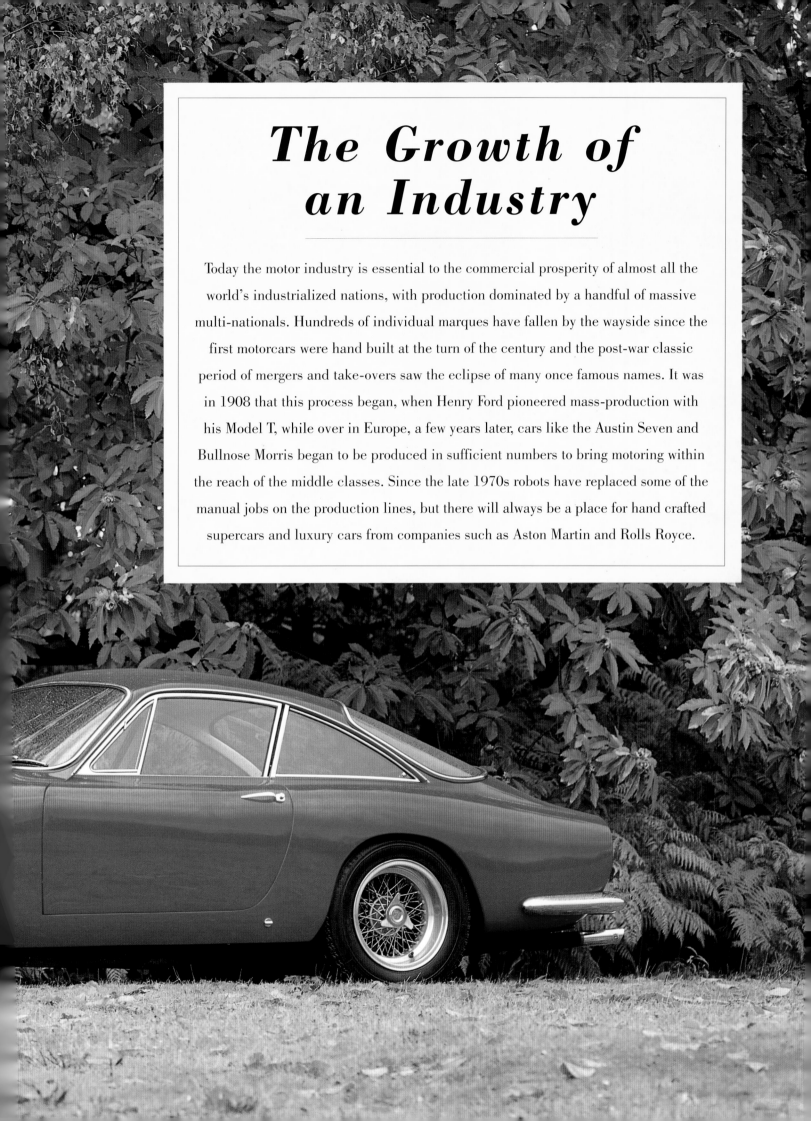

The Growth of an Industry

Today the motor industry is essential to the commercial prosperity of almost all the world's industrialized nations, with production dominated by a handful of massive multi-nationals. Hundreds of individual marques have fallen by the wayside since the first motorcars were hand built at the turn of the century and the post-war classic period of mergers and take-overs saw the eclipse of many once famous names. It was in 1908 that this process began, when Henry Ford pioneered mass-production with his Model T, while over in Europe, a few years later, cars like the Austin Seven and Bullnose Morris began to be produced in sufficient numbers to bring motoring within the reach of the middle classes. Since the late 1970s robots have replaced some of the manual jobs on the production lines, but there will always be a place for hand crafted supercars and luxury cars from companies such as Aston Martin and Rolls Royce.

WHAT MAKES A CLASSIC?

"Without a certain amount of snobbery, efforts would be hopeless ... A motorcar must be designed and built that is a little different from and a little better than the product of the big quantity manufacturer."

Cecil Kimber, founder of MG, had it right. He sensed a need and virtually invented the concept of the classic – but MGs have never been particularly special or mechanically innovative. What they do have, however, is that little extra desirability, so that owners and onlookers alike *see* them as classic cars. MGs are instantly recognizable, even to many non-enthusiasts, in much the same way that Jaguars, Ferraris and Bentleys are – all of them true classics.

Most enthusiasts would categorize a classic car as one whose design is inalienably right: it must look good, handle well, probably be possessed of higher performance or equipment

■ BELOW LEFT *BMW 328: a timeless classic, lithe, lean and light.*

■ ABOVE *Performance, grace - and a competition classic. NUB 120 is the most famous Jaguar XK120 ever.*

■ ABOVE *The basic shape of the Porsche 911 endured for nearly 35 years from launch in 1964.*

levels than were normal for its day – but overall it must be desirable.

Age alone cannot make a classic, even though a common definition given today is "any car more than 20 years old". Those who use that definition would say that Avengers and Marinas are classics; most enthusiasts with other criterior would not.

Beauty is in the eye of the beholder but there is no disputing the beauty of a real classic. Who cannot be moved by the shape and form of a Bugatti Type 35, Alfa Monza,

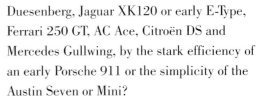

■ LEFT *Bugatti Type 35,*
a GP racer for the road
- a model of sparse
functional character.

Duesenberg, Jaguar XK120 or early E-Type,
Ferrari 250 GT, AC Ace, Citroën DS and
Mercedes Gullwing, by the stark efficiency of
an early Porsche 911 or the simplicity of the
Austin Seven or Mini?

Then there were the "firsts", each with its
claim to classicdom: Colin Chapman's Lotus
Seven, a racer for the road; the Mini Cooper 'S'
which further defined the small car and was
the first "pocket rocket"; the Hispano-Suiza
and Pegaso, Spain's only, exquisitely made
supercars from the 20s and 50s respectively;
the Reliant Scimitar GTE which introduced a
new concept – the sporting estate car; the Golf
GTi, which spawned a whole new breed of
enthusiasts' car. Each of these counts as a
classic for defining a new niche in car-lovers'
hearts. That each one of these cars – and many
more like them – is notable in its own field
helps reinforce its claim to be a true classic.

■ ABOVE *Duesenberg:*
coachbuilt elegance,
American style. It could
achieve more than
100mph (160kph).

■ RIGHT *The straight*
eight engined Alfa
Monza: epitome of the
classic vintage racer.

CLASSIC ENGINES

Once a classic is in motion, the engine does more than any other feature to give it character. The 1945–75 period started with almost universal use of sidevalve power, except on the most costly and exotic cars, and ended with multiple camshafts and valves, fuel injection and unusual materials becoming the norm. Most of these advances were first developed for racing, then refined for road use as they showed the way to efficiency.

Progress had meant more performance. Where 1940s power outputs were small, by the 70s, engines in better sportscars were up to 80bhp per litre. Efficiency came from ideally-shaped combustion chambers, usually hemispherical, for which a more complex valve arrangement is usually needed. The simplest way to operate these is by overhead cams, first seen on a Clément of 1902 and used by Alfa Romeo, Bentley and Bugatti in the 20s, MG in the 30s and Jaguar since the 50s, but not used on non-classics until the 80s. It's costly to develop but usually leads to better breathing.

Further advances included fuel injection,

■ ABOVE *The 16-cylinder powerplant used in the racing BRM: fantastically powerful, but too complicated to live.*

■ LEFT *The fearsome V-twelve of the racing Sunbeam Tiger. Aero engines were a convenient route to high power.*

■ BELOW LEFT *The light-alloy 3.5-litre Rover V-eight, beloved of specialist sportscar makers, is derived from an unwanted Buick unit of the 1960s.*

which did away with compromises forced by carburettors. It was first used on production cars, in rather basic form, by Chevrolet on its Corvette in 1954 and by Mercedes-Benz on its technical tour de force 300SL in 1955. In the early 70s, Bosch's Jetronic systems began to appear on performance classics such as the Porsche 911. Since 1993, with universal fitment of catalytic convertors, fuel injection has become a necessity, along with electronic ignition, which began to appear at the end of the 60s. For convenience, the hydraulic tappet was designed by Bollée in 1910. General Motors began to fit them in the 30s, leading to extra mechanical refinement and less servicing.

Hydraulic tappets were universal in America by the 60s; now almost all cars use them. These are the milestone power units:-

Jaguar XK

The XK was designed in the Second World War by the nicknamed "Firewatchers" Walter Hassan, Harry Mundy and Bill Heynes when they were on evening fire duty. It is the epitome of the classic in-line twin-cam engine and was sorely needed as an alternative to the pedestrian Standard engines Jaguar was forced

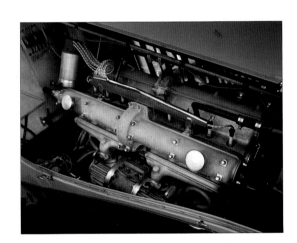

to use before and immediately after the war. Launched in the XK120 of 1948, displacing 3.4 litres and producing 160bhp, it enjoyed its finest moment in a road car as the 265bhp 3.8 which propelled the 1962 E-Type coupé to 150mph (241kph). In 3.0- and 3.4-litre dry-sumped form it took D-Types to Le Mans wins and powered Jaguar saloons right up to 1987.

Rover V-eight

A cast-off from Buick (the Americans had found themselves good at thin-wall iron casting so there was no need for fancy light-alloy stuff), this 3528cc engine was discovered by Maurice Wilks on a visit to America in 1966. Realizing

■ ABOVE *Classic Italian – the Maserati 250F V-twelve racing engine with twin camshafts and a separate carburettor choke for each cylinder.*

■ LEFT *Alfa Romeo's 2.9-litre engine of the 1930s used a twin double-overhead-camshaft, straight-eight layout.*

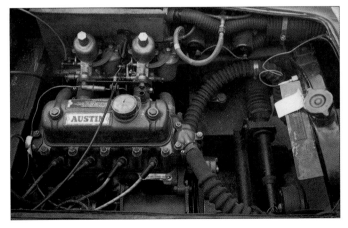

■ LEFT *For the Mini, the engine was cleverly turned sideways and integrated with the gearbox to produce a compact powerplant.*

■ ABOVE *Here's the same A-series engine, which first appeared in 1952, as it started out, mounted longitudinally.*

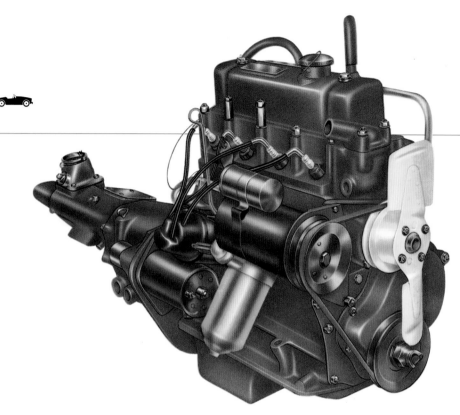

■ ABOVE *The B-series – bigger brother to the Mini engine – as used in the Wolseley 1500. It grew up to be a 1798cc unit powering the MGB.*

this compact unit would be perfect for powering Rover's big P5 saloon, he quickly acquired the rights. It was a good move: the staid, heavy saloon was transformed into one with a top speed of 110mph (177kph) and 0–60 (96) in 10 seconds. The engine did sterling service in the Rover 3500 before proving itself ideal for the Range Rover of 1970. Light and tunable, this engine has also found favour with MG, TVR, Marcos – and survives in 4.6-litre form in the Range Rover of 1996.

Ferrari V-twelve

Complex, beautifully made and exquisitely finished, Ferrari's engines are expensively engineered for big power at huge revs. The V-twelve was first seen in 1946 as the tiny Colombo-designed two-litre V-twelve 166. The larger Lampredi-designed engine appeared in 1951, in the 340 America. In front-engined Ferrari V-twelve parlance, the model number gives the displacement of one cylinder; multiply by 12 and you have the engine size. The four-camshaft layout arrived with the 275GTB/4 of 1966. This classic sports-car power unit looks as good as it goes: almost always with twin oil filters nestling together at the front of the vee and black crackle-finish cam covers cast with the legend "Ferrari".

Porsche flat-six

One of the longest-lived engines ever, this air- and oil-cooled flat six was derived from the flat four first seen pre-war in the VW Beetle. It grew from the 120bhp two-litre of 1963 to a turbocharged 3.3-litre, punching out a seamless

■ LEFT *The Cosworth DFV. Funded by Ford, this engine won over 100 Grands Prix.*

■ RIGHT *Lessons learned with the DFV spawned a whole series of Cosworth race engines. This is a four-cylinder BDA, showing the cogged belt which drives the twin camshafts.*

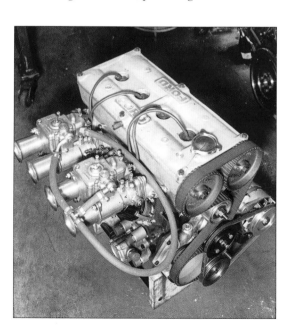

■ ABOVE *The rotary engine, used by Mazda and NSU, is so compact that it is almost hidden by its ancillaries.*

■ RIGHT *The mighty Cobras were all powered by the Ford V-eight of 4.2, 4.7 or 7 litres, producing up to 400bhp.*

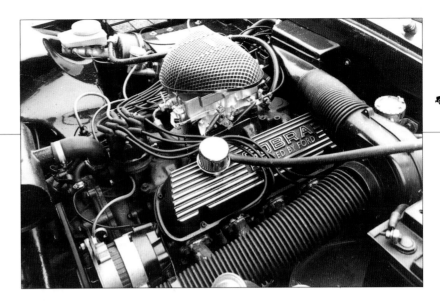

output with the low engine weight he needed for his small sportscars, it made sense to base this hitherto prohibitively expensive arrangement on existing engine technology. Ford's simple, light and tough 1340cc Kent engine from the short-lived Capri was the ideal candidate. For it, *Autocar's* then technical editor Harry Mundy designed a light-alloy twin-cam head with hemispherical combustion chambers and near-perfect valve angles. When Ford announced that the base pushrod engine would be enlarged to 1600cc form Chapman's new engine displaced 1558cc and produced 105bhp on twin carburettors. It has appeared in the Elan, the Europa, Lotus Cortinas and even early Escorts and inspired many followers.

300bhp with so much torque that only a four-speed gearbox was needed. Pioneering the Nikasil cylinder lining that did away with iron liners, and always with a single camshaft per cylinder bank, these exactingly engineered powerplants have a Germanic reputation for reliability and longevity. In the most classic 911 of all, the RS Carrera of 1973, it produces 210bhp at 7000rpm on mechanical fuel injection – accompanied by raw exhaust snarl that tingles the spine. A derivative still powers the current 911.

■ ABOVE *The two-litre four-cylinder Standard engine used in the Triumph TR3 also powered Vanguards, Morgans and, in modified form, the Ferguson tractor.*

■ RIGHT *The other side of the B series, as used in twin-carburettor 68bhp form in the Riley 1.5. The carburettor and exhaust are on the same side as the engine.*

Lotus/Ford twin-cam

When Colin Chapman realized in the 60s that twin camshafts were the way to achieve higher

SUSPENSION

The first suspension for cars – the most classically simple arrangement of all – was copied from horse-drawn carts. The beam axle, held to the chassis by leaf springs, is the simplest form of springing. It's still used, in little-modified form, on many of today's trucks. The system was used on the most basic cars until the 50s, and at the rear end of many cheaper cars until the 80s.

Soon, however, with increasing engine sophistication and speed, cart springs put limits on a car's ability to ride well and handle safely. By 1924, makers like Frazer Nash were trying extra links to control the axle's movement better while still springing it by leaf. The next big move was to independent suspension – where the movement of one wheel does not affect the other. Most of the world's favourite classic cars have this in some form but the way suspension is arranged seems to be national preference.

Americans were keen on independent front suspension by wishbones from the 1930s. An American invented the now universal MacPherson strut, although it was first used on a British car, the Ford Consul, in 1950.

Germans pioneered independent suspension

■ LEFT *The front suspension of the MG Magnette uses coil springs and double wishbones and is steered by rack and pinion.*

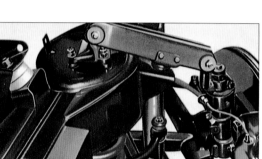

■ LEFT *Rover used a similar but larger system for its P4, this time with an anti-roll bar and separate, telescopic shock absorbers.*

■ LEFT *Mercedes used air suspension to provide a supple ride on its big 600 and 300SEL 6.3 saloons. A compressor inflates rubber bags incorporated between suspension members.*

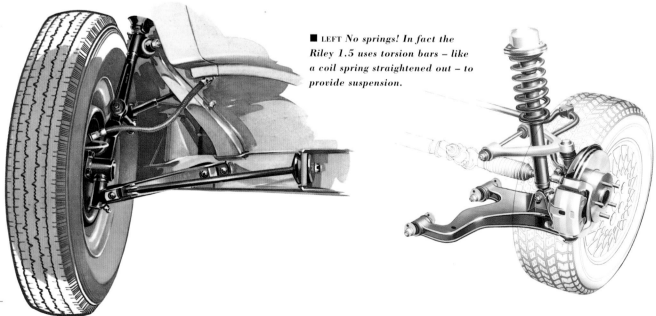

■ LEFT *No springs! In fact the Riley 1.5 uses torsion bars – like a coil spring straightened out – to provide suspension.*

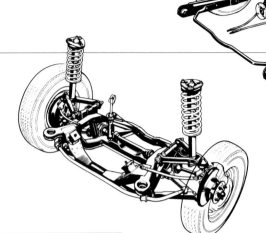

■ LEFT *Mounting the coil spring and damper concentrically solves a space problem but makes removal more complicated.*

■ ABOVE AND LEFT *Struts can be used to provide independent suspension at the front or rear.*

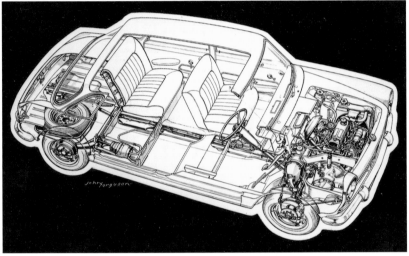

■ ABOVE *The Austin/Morris 1800 used Hydrolastic (fluid/air) suspension. One Hydrolastic unit can be seen under the cut-away rear seat.*

■ OPPOSITE *The modern solution is to suspend the car on struts, which incorporate both spring and damper. A MacPherson strut also locates and steers the wheel.*

by swing axles with the Mercedes, which lasted into the 60s. VW used a pair of trailing links, in parallel on each side of the car, for independent front suspension for the Beetle, which had a semiswing axle rear suspension. The typical set-up to be found on a performance saloon of the 60s and 70s consisted of MacPherson struts at the front and semitrailing arms at the rear. With liftoff or extreme power oversteer (tail slides) easily available, this produced what most enthusiasts would count as "classic" handling. The tail-heavy Porsche 911 and all BMWs of the 60s and 70s that were equipped with semitrailing arms tended to oversteer.

The Italian Fiat Topolino was ingeniously sprung by lower wishbones, transverse leaf springs, forming the upper links. Lancia used the same set-up in the 60s at the front of its

Fulvia and Flavia models and it could be found under Fiat-drive Seats of the 80s.

The purest and most classic suspension system of all, however, is the double wishbone set-up, used by practically all single-seat racing cars since the 50s and on most supercars thereafter. It's costly to make and can be tricky to set up correctly but offers the best fully-independent wheel control thanks to its ideal geometry and acceptable unsprung weight.

MacPherson struts

Ford's slab-sided new Consul of 1950 broke new ground with its full-width body hiding a new suspension system that revolutionized the way cars were built. An American Ford engineer, Earle S. MacPherson, came up with a new design for independent suspension whose beauty lay in its simplicity. MacPherson struts were used on every new small Ford – including the Classic of 1961 – and are the most common front suspension system used today.

Air suspension

Air suspension was tried by Cadillac on the 1958 Brougham and by Mercedes on its 300 and 600 saloons of the 60s. Air suspension provides a truly supple ride but air-bag durability, a fall in handling precision and the fact that modern, computer-controlled suspension is better made it a blind alley.

BRAKES AND TYRES

The first brakes were blocks of wood made to rub against wheel rims by a system of levers. This is how Trevithick's steamer of 1804 was slowed. As a method of stopping, it was woefully inadequate even for horse-drawn transport.

The 1886 Daimler used a wire hawser wrapped around a wooden ring mounted to the wheel hub. Pulling a lever tightened the wire, which slowed the rotating drum. A refinement of this was the use of a flexible steel band lined with wooden blocks or a strip of leather. This increased the brake's efficiency by extending its friction area.

In 1901, Maybach introduced the internally-expanding drum brake. It used a ring of friction material pressed against the inside of a brake drum by rollers. This was used on the 1903 Mercedes 40hp. Meanwhile, in 1902, Louis Renault designed the definitive drum brake still used today.

Renault's brake used two curved shoes fixed to a backplate, each pivoted at one end. The other ends rested on a cam. When the brake pedal was pressed, the cam forced the shoes

■ ABOVE *Disc brakes work by squeezing the rotor (the round bit) between a pair of friction pads which are fixed into the caliper (the lumpy bit).*

■ ABOVE LEFT *A very early Girling disc brake, as fitted to the TR3 from 1956. The pads were bolted in place.*

■ ABOVE *Power brakes were something to shout about in the 1940s; now nearly all cars have servo assistance.*

■ ABOVE *The next development was easier replacement of brake pads. On this 1959 Lockheed caliper, the pads are retained by pins.*

■ ABOVE *Drum brakes work by forcing the curved shoes against the inside of a drum, which rotates with the road wheel. They do not stand up to repeated stops as well as disc brakes.*

apart and against the inside of the drum.

Drum brakes served for 50 years. Initially, they were used on rear wheels only, for it was feared front brakes could cause skids. Mercedes was the first maker to fit four-wheel brakes, but only as an option, in 1903. All-wheel braking did not become a universal fitting until the 20s. Ever-increasing power and speed demanded more powerful drum brakes, which meant larger and wider. The ultimate form was the huge twin-leading shoe drums used by the Auto-Union and Mercedes "silver arrows" racing cars just before the Second World War. These incorporated scoops and fins

for maximum ventilation to keep temperatures moderate and reduce brake fade. When friction material becomes too hot, it stops working.

Discs take over

Nothing bettered these until Jaguar turned the brake world on its head with the disc brakes it pioneered on its C-Types at Le Mans in 1953. Crosley in America had tried discs in 1949 but soon stopped production. Jaguar gave discs worldwide acceptance. These brakes, borrowed from the aircraft industry, use a pair of friction pads to grip and slow a disc mounted to and spinning with the wheel hub. Because they dissipate heat better and are far more resistant to fade, they give much more powerful stopping for longer than drum brakes. Jaguar won the race that year. There was no going back. By 1956, Girling disc brakes were a standard fitment to Triumph's new sportscar, the TR3,

■ ABOVE *The Dunlop Road Speed RS5 – a crossply that was the performance choice if you had a big, powerful car in the 1950s.*

■ ABOVE *The Michelin XM+S – a "mud and snow" radial designed for severe winter conditions. It was fitted as standard to early Range Rovers.*

■ ABOVE *The Pirelli P600, an update of the legendary P6, was the performance tyre of the 1980s – here it's on a Golf GTi wheel. As well as having superb grip, its classic tread pattern also looked good.*

and the Jensen 541 had Dunlops. Jaguar offered Dunlop disc brakes as an option that year on its XK140. Every model since has had all-round discs as standard.

By the time four-wheel drum brakes were standardized at the end of the 20s, they operated by cables, rods and levers, or hydraulics, or a combination of both. Austin's Hydro-mechanical system, used on its small cars of the 40s and 50s, operated front brakes by hydraulics and rear by a system of rods. The MG Magna sportscar of the 30s had brakes operated by a system of cross-linkages and cables which needed frequent adjustment. The Americans had been using hydraulics since the Chrysler 58 of 1926. Citroën had its own ideas. Since the revolutionary DS of 1955, its cars have had fully-powered disc brakes all round. This gives powerful braking with light pedal pressure. Rolls-Royce used Citroën's high-pressure braking system for its Silver Shadow first seen in 1965.

The classic supercar brake setup, of servo-assisted, multipiston calipers gripping a ventilated disc brake at each wheel, has not been bettered. Antilock brakes – derived from aircraft technology – were pioneered in production on the four-wheel drive Jensen FF in 1966. They were not generally available until the 80s.

Tyres

The classic tyre always seems to be a bit wider and fatter than those on a modern car. Since cars began, the trend has been for fatter and stickier tyres. But it's the high-performance, most costly cars – the classics – that get them first. Crossply tyres, tall, unstylish, inflexible and short on grip, hung on into the 60s, but the classic tyres have all been radials.

CLASSIC STYLE

Body styling, the car's skin, is the emotional trigger that attracts most of us to a motorcar: driving it comes later, to seal the love affair – or end it. A pretty but underachieving car will always have more followers than one that drives like a dream but doesn't look like one.

1945–55

Many mass-produced cars were still tall and spindly. They had separate headlights and mudguards and narrow, letter-box screens.

In Italy, however, coachbuilder Battista "Pinin" Farina (later Pininfarina) had not been idle. His pre-war aerodynamic bodywork on the Lancia Aprillia chassis hinted at the disappearance of the separate wing profile within fully enveloping sides. With the Cisitalia 202 and Maserati 1500 Berlinetta, the theme found full expression. Simple and slender, these cars inspired a generation to come, including the beautiful Lancia Aurelia B20 of 1950, the first of the modern Gran Turismo coupés and a masterpiece of its period. Pininfarina styled many of the great Ferraris too, but it was Touring's classic 166 Barchetta, a model of elegant simplicity, that got the ball rolling in 1948. It directly influenced the AC Ace of

■ ABOVE *The 1951 Hudson, nicknamed "Step-down" for its low-slung construction.*

■ RIGHT *The classic Pininfarina-styled Cisitalia 202 coupé, a landmark.*

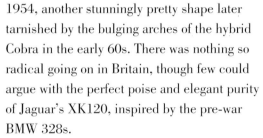

■ BELOW *The BMW 503 had clean, well-balanced lines that influenced BMW coupés of the 1960s and 1970s.*

1954, another stunningly pretty shape later tarnished by the bulging arches of the hybrid Cobra in the early 60s. There was nothing so radical going on in Britain, though few could argue with the perfect poise and elegant purity of Jaguar's XK120, inspired by the pre-war BMW 328s.

It was in America that some of the most influential, if not the best, styling would be created over the next decade or so. By 1948, the Americans were starting to shake off the pre-war left-overs and were shaping some radical cars: Ford's Custom series brought with it the new all-enveloping styling – later imitated on the British MkI Ford Consul/Zephyr series – while the "step-down" Hudson Super Six looked rakishly low and modern. The first tiny rear fins were beginning to appear on the Series

■ BELOW *A Studebaker by industrial designer Raymond Loewy.*

■ BELOW *An Austin A40, one of the Farina-styled British cars of the 1950s and 1960s.*

■ BELOW *Big American cars of the 1950s could retain elegance, as with this Cadillac.*

62 Cadillacs, a taster of what was to come.

It was Europe's sportscars that Americans were developing a real taste for by the early 50s: the 1953 Healey 100/4 was undeniably attractive, with a simple, perfectly balanced shape that was to survive 15 years. The TR2 was bug-eyed and awkward by contrast, yet enormously successful.

1955–65

The American influence was still strong during this period as the separate mudguard all but disappeared in the name of full-bodied, all-enveloping modernity. The trend was towards lower, wider cars. Chrome was still used in abundance but glass areas increased, hand in hand with half-framed doors and dog-leg wrap-around screens. In Britain, coach-building was

■ ABOVE *Bertone's Alfa Guilia, an early GT car.*

■ BELOW *Pininfarina was also responsible for the clean, elegant styling of the Lancia Flaminia coupé.*

still a lively trade as big luxury cars – mostly those of Rolls-Royce and Bentley – still had separate chassis construction, but this decade was to see many famous old names – even Rolls-Royce – switch to unitary construction which didn't really allow for coachbuilt bodywork.

Pininfarina took the styling initiative in the second half of the 50s with the Lancia Florida show car. Like the Cisitalia nine years earlier, here was a true turning point in design. The Florida's taut, chisel-edged architecture was set to influence big-car styling for decades (the 1957 Lancia Flaminia saloon came closest to original expression). An even more radical big saloon was Citroën's DS of 1955, a car that was as futuristic in looks as it was in technical detail. Another frontrunner in the beauty stakes was the 507 of 1955 from BMW, styled by Albrecht Goertz. Created to capture American sales and to challenge the 300SL Mercedes, it was always too expensive, but its slender,

was never designed to win catwalk prizes. Yet the boxy shape was so right and so eternally fashionable (and has changed so little) that it surely deserves a styling accolade.

Pininfarina – a big fan of the Mini – was virtually Ferrari's official stylist by the end of the 50s, shaping such classics as the Spider California, the 250 GT and countless show-stopping one-offs. He never got it more right

pinched-waist design remains one of the greats.

The Americans were on the verge of the tail-fin craze at this point, particularly General Motors designs. Under styling supremo Harley Earl, everything from the humble Chevrolet Bel Air upwards had rocket-inspired fins by 1957.

In Britain the second half of the 50s brought MG's pretty A roadster, the best-looking car they ever built, while Lotus was about to break into the mainstream with the delicate Elite, a timelessly elegant little coupé. Meanwhile, Bertone of Italy built the first of its memorable, long-lived Giulietta Sprint Coupés in 1955, offered with a Pininfarina Spider version.

Form came second to function with the revolutionary Mini Minor of 1959, so the car

■ ABOVE *One of the most mouthwatering Ferraris ever, the 250 Lusso.*

■ RIGHT *The Facel Vega combining Italianate good looks with V-eight power was French.*

■ BELOW *Lancia Stratos, brutal but beautiful, derived from a Bertone show car. Fewer than 1,000 were built.*

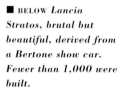

than with the 250 Berlinetta Lusso: here was a compact two-seater with perfect proportions.

Much the same could be said of Jaguar's sensational E-Type roadster and coupé launched at Geneva in 1961. Malcolm Sayers's slim and sensual design was a lesson in motorcar archi-tecture, derived from his D-Type racer of the mid-50s. American styling was finding its way again in the early 60s with clean, well-propor-tioned cars like the Corvair, the Studebaker Avanti and the Buick Riviera coupé. The 1961 Lincoln "Clap door" Continental was Detroit styling at its most elegant.

1965–75
The tailfin had all but disappeared by 1965 and even the Americans were cleaning up their act with handsome, clean-lined, if still huge, cars. The fuss and clutter of 50s saloon cars was being swept away by cleaner, classier styling,

boxy at worst (e.g. the Fiat 124), elegant at best.

In Europe, Bertone was a force in the mid-60s, its crowning glory the magnificent mid-engined Miura. Bertone made waves with the Lamborghini Espada, too, although it was cleverly conceived rather than beautiful in the conventional sense, a big four-seater coupé with a bold, uncompromising profile. With the introduction of the Ghia-styled Ghibli in 1965, Maserati finally had a supercar to challenge Ferrari. Conventionally front-engined, it was every bit as beautiful as the Miura, cleaving the air with a sharply-profiled snout.

The Ferrari Dino 206 of 1967 was the finest-looking car Pininfarina had launched for some time, a jewel-like mid-engined coupé that survived well into the 70s. The 1967 NSU Ro80 was certainly the most futuristic production saloon of the decade, its rising waistline, tall glasshouse and low prow prophetic of aerodynamic saloons yet to come.

Jaguar proved they could still build a good-looking car with the wide, curvy XJ6 of 1968, a classic shape that was to prove very durable: it was still being made in 1990. The trendsetter of 1968, however, came from Staffordshire, in the English Midlands, in the shape of the Reliant Scimitar GTE, the first sporting estate car.

Citroën made a dramatic start to the 70s with a swoopy glass-nosed coupé called the SM.

Here was a real piece of automotive sculpture with presence and enormous class. Fiat's classic 130 coupé was more chisel-edged, its glass-to-steel areas perfectly balanced with wonderful detailing and fine, sharp lines.

Though many beautiful cars have been made since the mid-70s, it is only when the passage of years has allowed us to see them in the context of their time and ours that the truly classic shapes will emerge.

■ ABOVE LEFT *Alfa Romeo Montreal - a front-engined supercar with mid-engined looks.*

■ ABOVE RIGHT *Spen King's Range Rover was the first luxury offroader in 1970. Its classic lines remained in production for 25 years.*

■ LEFT *Alfa's 2000 coupé was an enduring design by Bertone.*

BODYWORK CONSTRUCTION

Car bodywork followed horse-carriage procedure until the 1920s – in style and construction. With the first cars and until the start of the 50s on prestige cars like Rolls-Royce and Bentley, the customer chose throughout – buying first the rolling chassis from the maker, then having it bodied in a selected style by a chosen coachbuilder.

A typical light or sporting car of the 20s would have had fabric body panels stretched over a wooden frame – with aluminium used to form the bonnet and wings. Notable examples were Weymann bodies and classic Vanden Plas

■ LEFT *Fiat's Topolino featured an all-steel one-piece body. It was one of the first small cars so built.*

■ ABOVE *Le Mans Bentley: ash frame, fabric covering and an aluminium bonnet.*

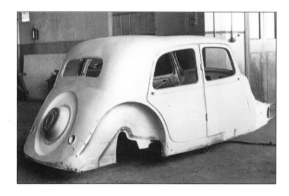

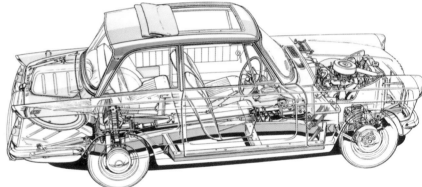

■ ABOVE *A cutaway of the Triumph Herald showing its separate chassis.*

■ LEFT *The Citroën Traction Avant's monocoque (one-piece) body exposed. Front outriggers supported the powertrain.*

■ BELOW LEFT *"Skeleton" of a unitary-construction steel body. Outer panels will be welded or bolted in place.*

open-tourer bodies used on Bentleys. Even when aluminium was later used for all the outer panels, the traditional ash frame remained underneath until the advance of machine-pressed steel panels which could be welded together. The BSA of 1912 was one of the first cars to use this construction. Soon, it was adopted for all small cars, leading to a standardization of body styles. But bodies were still built separately and then mounted on to a chassis which held all the mechanicals. Surely, it would be simpler and more efficient to build the body and chassis as one? Vincenzo Lancia thought so and his beautiful Lancia Lambda of

■ RIGHT *Superleggera (superlight) bodies are made by clothing a lightweight tubular frame in steel or aluminium panels.*

■ FAR RIGHT *The Lotus Elan's backbone chassis holds all major mechanical components. The glass-fibre body slips over the top.*

1923 was the world's first monocoque passenger car. Monocoque means all or most of the loads are taken by the car body's skin. It took a while, however, for other makers to catch up. The VW Beetle of 1938 was a half-way house, relying on the body being bolted on top to provide full rigidity. It was Citroën's revolutionary front-wheel-drive *Traction-avant* of 1934 which popularized the monocoque. Full unitary construction, where the chassis and body are made in one shell with openings for doors and windows, came along with the Ford Consul in 1950. This is the way nearly all cars have been built since.

Superleggera

In this construction, thin steel tubes are built up from the floorpan or chassis, into the shape of the finished body. Aluminium panels are then painstakingly formed by hand (rolled between shaped wheels, or beaten over a suitable wooden former, often a section of tree stump) until they fit the shape. They are then

welded together over the frame. Most Ferraris and Maseratis were built this way until the end of the 1950s; the Aston Martin DB4, 5 and 6 were Superleggera cars, too.

Glass fibre (Lotus and Corvette)

Glassfibre is light and easy to work with but usually needs a separate chassis underneath to carry all heavy mechanicals. The Lotus Elan of 1962 is a good example: the one-piece glass-fibre body of this classic small sportscar sits over a simple Y-shaped pressed- and welded-steel backbone. Originally, the Elan was intended to have a much more complicated chassis, but designer Ron Hickman drew up the simple steel chassis as a temporary measure so development on the rest of the car could continue. It stayed. The first glass-fibre-bodied car was the classic Chevrolet Corvette of 1953.

Lotus Elite (glass fibre monocoque)

This car has no steel in the body and chassis, except for localized strengthening. All the stresses are taken through the one-piece (monocoque) body and floorpan unit. Production and budget troubles almost caused Lotus to go under, and Chapman's next car was the more conventional Elan.

■ BELOW *The Lotus Elite was the first glass-fibre monocoque body. It had steel strengthening bonded in at all key points to mount the suspension.*

THE INDUSTRY, 1945–55

After the Second World War, factories that had been used to make aircraft, aero engines and munitions were turned back to car making. Such had been the industry's preoccupation with war work, however, that there were no new car designs. If you could afford a new car, a pre-war design was what you got, such as Ford's Prefect, which started production in 1938. Even these were in short supply on the home market, for the Government's message to put the economy on its feet was "export or die".

In Germany, production of the KdF Wagen, or "Strength through Joy" car, which became known as the VW Beetle, had got under way again after a faltering pre-war start. Hitler's pre-war dream was for Germany to make a car that every family could afford; in a shattered post-war country, it took the British Army's Royal Electrical and Mechanical Engineers, under Major Ivan Hurst, to get Ferry Porsche's inspired design back into production in post-war Germany.

Later in the 1950s, former aircraft producer Messerschmitt made its own idea of cheap transport for the masses, an alternative to the motorcycle, in its KR200, a tandem two-seater with an aircraft-style canopy and a tiny two-stroke engine in the rear. Today, these cars,

which look like fighter planes on three wheels, are much prized. BMW, trying to keep its head above water now that few of its aircraft engines were needed, tried a different but equally humble route: the Isetta "bubblecar".

Britain thought it needed to earn money after the war with a "world car" for export. A first all-new British design was the Standard Vanguard of 1947, intended to take on the Americans and Australians in their markets. But the most successful export was the Land-Rover of 1948, designed by Rover's Maurice Wilks as a farm runabout and based on a Jeep

■ ABOVE *Typical British cars of the 1950s were small and austere, such as Ford's Popular and Anglia.*

■ LEFT *This 1953 Buick typifies America and the cars it made in the 50s - big and brash.*

■ RIGHT *The Standard Vanguard was Britain's idea of a "world car".*

■ LEFT *The Wilks brothers' Land-Rover brought utility vehicles to the masses, courtesy of the Jeep.*

■ ABOVE *The "people's car", the VW Beetle, still in production - in Mexico - in 1997.*

chassis, after the Jeep he used on his farm wore out. The Morris Minor of the same year could have been a true world car if it had been marketed as aggressively as the Beetle. Its excellent handling and spritely performance guaranteed it true classic status – and it was Britain's first million-selling car. Ford remained true to its cheap, simple, slightly American-influenced but refined formula first

used for the monocoque-shelled, MacPherson-strutted Consul and continued with its successors through the 1950s.

Rolls-Royce, having taken over Bentley in 1931, continued its line of separate-chassis large saloons, its modern new Silver Cloud and sister Bentley S-Type with classical lines by in-house stylist John Blatchley that still have commanding presence.

In America, less badly affected by the war, car output continued unabated. Exciting, plush new models appeared every year. Even ordinary American passenger-cars offered labour-saving convenience items that would only be seen on luxury cars elsewhere. Citroën stunned the world with its futuristic and technically-advanced DS of 1955, but real innovations were still around the corner, and yet no one took Japan's increasing interest in car production seriously.

■ RIGHT *Messerschmidt 500 - the hot version. Most of these tandem two-seaters were 175 or 200cc.*

■ LEFT *An early advertisement for Maxis, and its Minor, Cowley, Oxford and Isis models.*

■ FAR LEFT *The German DKW had a two-stroke engine and front-wheel drive.*

MORRIS
raises the standard of motoring you can afford to enjoy

THE INDUSTRY, 1956–60

A new wave of post-Second World War optimism made the mid-50s an era of exciting new sportscars and saloons.

The "Big Healey" – the Austin-Healey 100, later the 3000 – had been with us since 1952 and the Chevrolet Corvette had appeared the next year. MG slotted its curvy new A in at sub-Healey level in 1955. Aston Martin's fast DB2/4 had metamorphosed into the three-litre DB MkIII by this period but was about to be superseded by 1958's DB4. That year along came a cheeky baby, the Austin-Healey Sprite. At first made with no boot lid and the raised headlamps that gave it the "Frogeye" nickname ("Bugeye" in America), this little car was mechanically an Austin A35.

The AC Ace had been in production from 1953 and a decade later formed the basis for one of the most infamous classics of all – the Cobra which appeared in 1962–63.

The Morgan 4/4 reappeared in 1956. In company nomenclature, this stood for four wheels and four cylinders, using Ford's 1172cc sidevalve engine. Other Morgans were powered by the two-litre TR3 unit. The only significant change was use of a cowled nose, rather than

the "flat radiator" style, from 1954.

The big Jaguar news was that the Coventry company complemented its big MkVII saloon with an exciting new compact. Sold initially with 2.4-litre power, it gained its claws as the

■ LEFT *The "fintail" saloons of the 1960s continued to build on Mercedes' reputation for longevity and excellence – the larger 220S in the background first appeared in 1959.*

■ BELOW LEFT *The oddly styled, air-suspended Borgward 2.3 is hardly remembered now, but in its day was a serious rival to Mercedes.*

■ BOTTOM LEFT *Ford's stylish Zodiac MkII was an update of the MkI and helped move technology forward with MacPherson struts and higher-revving engines.*

■ BOTTOM RIGHT *The "Auntie" Rover P4 stuck to traditional wood-and-leather values; later models like this 80 from 1960 were more conservatively styled than the first "Cyclops" 75 of 1950.*

MkII in 1959, with disc brakes and the 3.8-litre version of the XK straight six.

Ford's MkII Consul and Zephyr saloon arrived in 1956, essentially a slightly larger, restyled version of the MkI. Porsche's 356 continued to be improved with better engines. By 1960, 125mph (201kph) was available from the exotic, four-cam 356A Carrera.

In 1959 as American cars were getting bigger and flashier, Alec Issigonis stunned the world with his revolutionary new Mini. Fitting four adults into a 10-ft bodyshell is not easy, but he did it by exemplary packaging – putting in the engine sideways and mounting the gearbox underneath it so the powertrain used the shortest possible space, and fitting a small, 10-in wheel at each corner.

In 1958 the first two-box design and precursor of the hatchback, the Pininfarina-styled A40, appeared. Italian stylists were in vogue: 1959 saw the Michelotti-styled Triumph Herald, which was to give birth to the MG

■ ABOVE *The Austin Healey Sprite lost its "frog eyes" by 1961, and was joined by the identical, badge-engineered MG Midget. This is a 1275cc MkIV Sprite from 1968.*

■ ABOVE RIGHT *Like all proper (pre-Fiat take-over) Lancias, the Flaminia GT was gorgeous, superbly engineered – and expensive.*

■ BELOW LEFT *The Armstrong Siddeley Star Sapphire harked back to a golden age of British luxury saloons, but it was the last car the company made. Production finished in 1960.*

■ BELOW *Even the sporty MG Magnette saloon had its virtues extolled by exaggerated artwork.*

Midget competitor, the Spitfire, in 1962.

In Italy, Alfa Romeo was gearing up for true mass production with its boxy but highly competent Giulietta Berlina. Even more exciting was the Giulietta Sprint, styled by Bertone, a proper little GT that could run rings around many bigger sportscars. The mainstay of Fiat production was still the little rear-engined 500 and 600 models with a wide range of ultra-conventional rear-wheel-drive three-box saloons, from the little 1100 through to the sharp-edged 2100 six-cylinder cars. Lancia, though still losing money because of their obsession with tool-room standards of engineering, produced the most significant car of 1960 – the Flavia. Here was the first Italian car with front-wheel drive, a modern roomy body and superbly insulated suspension.

MAGNETTE MG SALOON

safety fast in airsmoothed style

THE INDUSTRY, 1961–75

For the British industry, the 1960s began successfully, but a series of mergers and takeovers and closure of several established British car-makers left it faltering by the decade's end.

The years of triumph had really begun in 1959 when the Mini appeared and, after the E-Type stunned the world at the Geneva Motor Show, other future classics emerged. There was Chapman's new Elan for 1962, closely following the Mini Cooper – a whole new breed of "pocket rocket", or hot small car. By this time, Ford's Cortina had also appeared; larger than

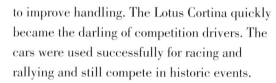

■ ABOVE *Cadillac was still making huge landcruisers in the 1960s but at least the fins were shrinking.*

■ LEFT *The 250 GTO was the last of Ferrari's front-engined racers.*

to improve handling. The Lotus Cortina quickly became the darling of competition drivers. The cars were used successfully for racing and rallying and still compete in historic events.

The 60s were the golden era for muscle cars in the USA. Cheap petrol meant there was no restraint on makers shovelling more and more horsepower into medium-sized saloons, a trend started with the Chrysler 300 series in 1955.

In Germany, NSU pioneered its futuristic new Ro80. Problems with its rotary power unit made it an engineering blind alley but the cars, when running, were amazingly good. Look how

■ RIGHT *NSU's Ro80 was far ahead of its time but engine-reliability problems killed it.*

the Austin 1100, the best-selling car for much of the 60s, it was simple, cheap and light and returned adequate performance from its modest 1200 and 1500cc engines. This car gave birth to a true classic when Colin Chapman got his hands on it, slotting in the twin-cam engine used in the Elan and sorting out the suspension

■ RIGHT *Germanic excellence is epitomized by the 928, a heavyweight grand tourer launched in 1970.*

■ ABOVE *Ford's Cortina 1600E opened up a new class of car, the sporty "executive saloon".*

■ ABOVE *Early 1970s muscle. This Chevrolet Camaro represents the peak years of the American "pony car".*

similar modern Audis are to that car now.

In 1962, the world saw one of the most sensual classics of all: the Ferrari GTO. Lightweight homologation specials and the last of Ferrari's front-engined racers, these cars are possibly the most desirable anywhere in the world today. Despite once being valued at up to £6 million each, many are still racing. Slightly more affordable was the 275GTB/4 of 1966, considered by some to be the best all-round Ferrari. Then in 1968, two of the most important and memorable of Ferrari's cars appeared – the heavyweight 365GTB/4 Daytona and the delicate mid-engined 246 Dino.

When the 1970s began, the British motor industry, was down to three major players: Leyland, Rootes and Ford. By now BMC was under the control of Leyland. Alvis had become part of Rover, which itself had been swallowed up by Leyland and thus found itself in the same group as its old rival, Jaguar, which had gone under the protective arm of BMC.

Elsewhere, news was brighter. The beautiful, shark-like Ferrari 308 GTB (a Dino replacement) appeared in 1975. In Germany, BMW had taken a lead in aerodynamics to produce one of the the most classic saloon racers of all time, the CSL. Porsche was just putting the final touches to turbocharging its 911. But for Britain, whose industry was by now on a three-day week and would never be the same again, all that emerged at the end of this period was Jaguar's disappointing XJS. 1975 was the dim end of a classic era.

■ ABOVE *The 1970s Wedge Princess showed how styling had lost its way. Such lame ducks helped nearly finish Britain's motor industry.*

■ BELOW LEFT *De Tomaso Panterra, an Italian supercar powered by Ford V-eight muscle.*

■ BELOW RIGHT *MGB - the classic roadster, launched in 1962. Everyone seems to have owned one...*

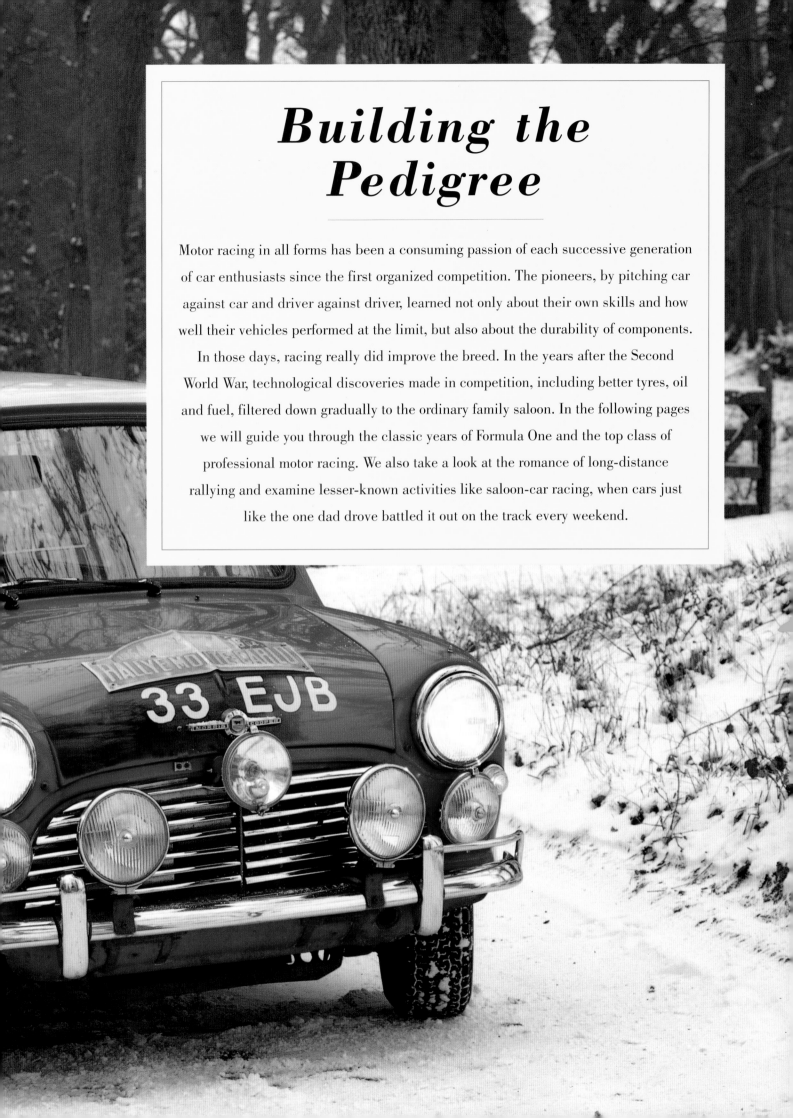

Building the Pedigree

Motor racing in all forms has been a consuming passion of each successive generation of car enthusiasts since the first organized competition. The pioneers, by pitching car against car and driver against driver, learned not only about their own skills and how well their vehicles performed at the limit, but also about the durability of components. In those days, racing really did improve the breed. In the years after the Second World War, technological discoveries made in competition, including better tyres, oil and fuel, filtered down gradually to the ordinary family saloon. In the following pages we will guide you through the classic years of Formula One and the top class of professional motor racing. We also take a look at the romance of long-distance rallying and examine lesser-known activities like saloon-car racing, when cars just like the one dad drove battled it out on the track every weekend.

GRAND PRIX

■ ABOVE *Colin Chapman's revolutionary Grand Prix cars put the driver in a monocoque "tub" with the engine behind him. Here a 25 heads up a Type 23 sports racer.*

As soon as two cars met, motor racing was invented. The first organized competition was the Paris–Bordeaux–Paris road race of 1895, won by Emile Levassor in a car of his own make. The average speed was 15mph (24kph), but by 1900, in a similar race from Paris to Lyons (Lyon), this rose to nearly 40mph (64kph). With little in the way of progress except lack of tyre technology, monster racing cars were soon thundering down dusty, unmade

roads at up to 100mph (160kph).

Racing on public roads did not last long. Fatalities in the 1903 Paris–Madrid and Gordon Bennett Trophy races created the need for dedicated circuits. The world's first, Brooklands, opened in 1907; in the 1920s and 30s heroes such as Birkin and the Bentley boys thundered around here and Le Mans. On these closed circuits, the need for riding mechanics was gone. Single-seater racing was born.

The golden age of racing

Think classic Grand Prix racer and you think 1930s Bugatti. But the greatest era of single-seater racing was the 50s. This was the golden age: with little to separate the crowds from the track apart from rows of straw bales, the racing

enthusiast could actually see his heroes at work, unfettered by high cockpit sides, full-faced helmets or the drivers' need to dress up as mobile billboards. While Fangio was still king of the hill on a good day and a quiet American called Phil Hill took his first drives with Ferrari, greats such as Stirling Moss, Peter

■ ABOVE LEFT *Heroic drivers set off at the start of the 1933 500 miles race at Brooklands, the first purpose-built racing track. The curved banking can clearly be seen in the distance.*

■ ABOVE *Stirling Moss, one of the world's greatest drivers, handles his Cooper 500 around a wet Silverstone in 1954.*

■ LEFT *Mike Hawthorn, one of the most charismatic drivers and Britain's first world champion, in 1958. He retired from racing in 1959.*

■ LEFT *Porsche 917s (20, 21, 22) get a strong start at the beginning of Le Mans, 1970. These cars took over from the Ford GT40s to dominate the 24-hour endurance race for much of the following decade.*

start, Alfa Romeo dominated the scene with the glorious Tipo 158 and 159, but Ferrari, BRM and Mercedes continued to push the tried and tested rear-engined formula, and Maserati's 250F – the classic racing car – won the hearts of drivers and spectators alike. Mercedes used its revolutionary W196 streamliners to steamroller the French Grand Prix at Reims (Rheims) in 1954. But it was Cooper which turned the racing world on its head by the end of the 50s with light, home-built rear-engined single-seaters.

The Chapman revolution

The man who had the greatest influence on Grand Prix cars and took racing-car design into the 60s, having started building his own cars in the 50s, was Colin Chapman. This structural engineer started racing with his Lotus Six and Seven (still with us as the Caterham Seven).

Collins and Mike Hawthorn were at the peaks of their careers – and remained great mates, too. Grand Prix racing had become so popular by the early 50s that crowds of 100,000 flooded to the two big races of the year at Silverstone. This ex-airfield circuit was the home of British motor racing and hosted the British Grand Prix and the British Empire Trophy. Even in those days, you had to be through Buckingham or Bicester by 7.30am to make the start – and little has changed.

This decade and the one after also saw the quickest evolution of racing machinery. At the

■ ABOVE *Mercedes' W154 "Silver Arrow" GP racer. Thorough engineering made these cars nigh-on invincible in the 1930s.*

■ RIGHT *Ford GT40. After Ford had failed to buy Ferrari it built its own cars to win Le Mans. They were successful in four consecutive years from 1966.*

■ BELOW RIGHT *The Lotus 78 Formula 1 car was one of the last of Colin Chapman's innovative designs.*

■ LEFT *One-off V12 version of the Maserati 250F, in six-cylinder form perhaps the greatest front-engined Grand Prix car the world has ever known.*

RALLYING FROM THE 50S TO THE 70S

Rallying in the 50s usually meant long-distance time trials where navigational accuracy and not necessarily outright speed was the criterion. Crews of two or three would battle through adverse conditions against an exhausting time schedule, armed with little more than standard cars upgraded only by extra lights and knobbly tyres. The most famous endurance events are the winter Monte Carlo and Alpine rallies where machinery as diverse as Sunbeam Rapiers, big and small saloons and sportscars, contemporary and vintage, competed against each other. Many entries would be "works" ones, from car makers anxious to prove their model's reliability. Later, in the 1960s, the Porsche 91 made its name as a durable car that withstood all that long-distance rallying could throw at it – and the 911 remains the car to beat in historic rallying in the 90s.

There were rallies at a local level, accessible to anyone who had a car and joined a motor club. These again were tests of navigational and timing accuracy, not speed, often at night.

■ LEFT *Tough hardtop saloons like the Ford Escort dominated rallying from the late 1960s.*

■ LEFT *Alpine rallies were tests of reliability, not outright speed.*

■ BOTTOM LEFT *The light, nimble Austin-Healey Sprite made a capable rally car.*

No helmets or elaborate safety procedures would be needed in those days when even such ungainly machinery as Austin A90 Atlantics would have had a chance.

Stage rallying

By the 70s, rallying to most people had come to mean "stage rallies". These are essentially a series of rough-road sprints. Cars blast sideways in crowd-pleasing power-slides, often on slippery shale or in treacherous ice conditions, through a narrow, twisty course accessible to spectators. The timed sections, or stages, range from a couple of miles to more than 30 (48km), and the object is to get down them as fast as

■ LEFT *The Austin-Healey 3000 in its element. This was one of the rally cars to have in the 1960s.*

■ LEFT *The Mini has been one of the most successful rally cars ever.*

■ ABOVE *A highly-modified Ford Escort being serviced on the 1970 London-Mexico rally.*

■ BELOW *Lancia Stratos, the Ferrari-powered purpose-built rally car, on a special stage.*

possible. The navigator's job is to get driver and car to the start of each stage at the right time, but in the frantic activity of negotiating the stage he is more than mere ballast. Using maps or "tulip" diagrams, he warns the driver of the severity of approaching corners, for advance reconnaissance has often been banned. Shrewd navigation is needed on the road sections between stages: these are subject to strict timing, too, and point loss is possible.

The premier event in Britain has always been the RAC Rally. By the end of the 60s the Ford Escort was king, driven by such stars as Roger Clark and the "Flying Finns", Timo Makinen and Ari Vatanen.

Classic 50s rally car – Austin-Healey

The durability of the powerful, separate-chassis two-seater Austin-Healey, launched in 1954, made it the favourite for long-distance rallies over the Alps. Its first successes were with the Morley brothers. Rally legend Timo Makinen first came to fame driving a "Big Healey". But there was tremendous noise from the bellowing, three-litre straight-six engine,

and lack of suspension movement made for poor ground clearance and a boneshaking ride.

First of the evolution specials – Stratos

With its show-car derived styling and Ferrari V-six engine, the Stratos was conceived with the sole purpose of winning rallies once Lancia's mainstay, the front-wheel-drive Fulvia, had aged. This twitchy, short-wheelbase homologation special (legend has it not even the requisite 500 were built) won the World Rally Championship three times, from 1974–76, and was forerunner of the short-lived, rally-specific Group B cars banned in 1986 for being too dangerous. The Stratos's last win was in the 1979 Monte Carlo Rally.

SALOON CAR RACING

Saloon racing has always been used by car makers – officially or not – to prove the excellence of their products. "Win on Sunday, sell on Monday" is the slogan. If Joe Public saw a car winning that he perceived as being like his own, then brand loyalty was strengthened and could even lead to new sales.

Saloon-car racing began soon after the Second World War, but, even well into the 50s, racing saloon cars were terrifyingly similar to their standard counterparts. Perhaps the tyres would be inflated, the hubcaps removed and a helmet worn, but there would be little safety gear until the 60s.

Professionals such as Graham Hill, who started in saloon cars and continued to race Jaguar MkIIs and Lotus Cortinas into the 60s, might wear overalls or at least matching polo shirt and trousers, but for the rest it would be everyday wear – taking a cue from 50s Grand Prix ace Mike Hawthorn who always raced in a sports jacket and bow-tie.

As new models came on stream, so they would be pressed into service on the tracks, becoming faster as more was learned about their tuning potential. The powerful MkI and MkII Jaguars, first seen in 1957, were naturals, as were to a lesser extent the six-cylinder Ford

■ ABOVE *Modern suspension and a light, stiff unitary body gave 50's Mk1 Ford Zephyrs a chance of success.*

■ BELOW LEFT *The humble Austin Westminster was surprisingly successful in 1950s saloon-car racing.*

■ BELOW RIGHT *Cars were surprisingly standard, hence alarming roll angles.*

Zephyr and Zodiac, but by the early 60s the Mini had started to creep on to the grid, aided by John Cooper of Formula 1 fame. The Mini was a landmark car in this respect; racing people who started their careers in Minis include Ken Tyrrell, James Hunt and the great John Rhodes whose tyre-smoking sideways cornering antics are legend. Others who enjoyed rattling around in unsuitable old cars included Stirling Moss and Jim Clark.

By the 60s, proper championships for touring and modified saloons had become

established, leading to exciting racing among Formula 2-engined Escorts, for example, and to the birth of the extensively modified saloons with the Group 2 and 4 BMW "Batmobiles" – and fearsome devices such as the series of Blydenstein Vauxhalls fielded in 70s "Supersaloon" racing by the larger-than-life Gerry Marshall.

America had evolved its own racing for "stock", or standard, saloons. This had started as a 200-mile (322km) sand/Tarmac race at Daytona Beach, Florida, in 1936. By 1959, the course had been transformed into a purpose-built two-mile (3.2km) banked oval track in the same location, and similar tracks sprang up all over the country under the auspices of NASCAR, the National Association for Stock Car Auto Racing. By the end of the 60s, "stock" cars were circulating at up to 200mph (322kph), aided by careful attention to aerodynamics and the rule book.

In Sports Car Club of America racing, where cars had to turn right as well as left, the AC Cobra/Corvette wars of the mid-60s gave way to multiround contests between modified Mustangs and Camaros, making heroes of men like Mark Donohue and Peter Revson.

Farther south, Mexico hosted the maddest road race ever, the 1,864 miles (3,000km) Carrerra Panamericana. This flat-out spectacle, which included a class for saloons among the diverse machinery taking part, was run annually from 1950 until 1954, when the growing number of fatalities forced closure. Since 1991, it has been run again as a retrospective road event.

■ **BELOW** *"Big Bertha", the V-eight-powered Vauxhall Ventura supersaloon built in the 1970s by Bill Blydenstein for the race ace Gerry Marshall to drive.*

CLASSICS IN COMPETITION TODAY

Classic motor sport has never been more popular. Purists think it's a shame to use up venerable old machinery, but the pragmatic say racing cars were built to race.

Historic motor sport doesn't have to mean big bucks or major track extravaganzas; there are plenty of gentler sprints, hill climbs or rallies populated by more modest machinery. Whatever the car, there's an extra-curricular activity you can do with it. Here are some of the activities that enthusiasts get up to with their classics.

Road runs

Not competition but open to anyone with a suitable classic (usually at least 20 years old) and a road licence, these are run by many clubs as a way of providing their major events with a focal point and also by large organizations such as the RAC MSA which runs the UK's largest annual road run.

Trials

You can enter a production-car trial in pretty much anything with four wheels – but the most stylish trials for classics are the ones operated by the Vintage Sports Car Club (VSCC), for cars made before 1930. The point of a trial is to arrive at the right place at the right time and to clear certain muddy hill climb sections without stopping. The winner is the driver with fewest errors.

Sprints and hill climbs

Within reason, you can sprint or hill climb any classic, vintage or veteran car you want. Only the most basic safety gear and the cheapest competition licence are needed. Each competitor embarks on two practice and two timed runs on a short, usually twisty course.

■ ABOVE *Historic endurance rallies, following the routes of the classic Alpine rallies of the '50s, are usually for cars made before 1962 and can easily be won in cars like this Jowett Jupiter: accuracy is the key, in both navigation and timing.*

■ ABOVE *Special-built post-war vintage racing combines Napier aero engine and Bentley chassis.*

■ ABOVE *Fast roads tours are available for more rarefied machinery on an invite-only level. Here an Alfa chases an HWM.*

■ ABOVE *Historic sports car racing has never gone away. Here a Cooper Monaco leads at Brands Hatch.*

■ BELOW *The famous paddock shelters at Shelsley Walsh near Worcester, where hillclimbs have been held since 1905.*

■ RIGHT *Historic Grand Prix cars, such as this Lotus, have a strong following, and more are being brought back to the race tracks all the time.*

Navigational rallies

Usually run at night, navigational rallies are tests of map-reading, navigation and time-keeping. Although they aren't speed events as such, an accurate average must be kept.

Stage rallies

There's some navigation in these events, but only to get the car to the beginning of each special stage in good time – and then all hell breaks loose. The stage, often on narrow forest gravel tracks, is closed to traffic, and the object is to get to the other end as fast as possible.

■ ABOVE *A supercharged MG tackles Shelsley, where competitors ascend the hill in less than a minute.*

■ BELOW *Like Lincoln's axe, many historic cars have had parts replaced, but have never stopped racing. Some are going faster than ever.*

Endurance rallies

From the three-day Monte Carlo Challenge over the snowy Alps to the 10-week London-Mexico, run in 1995 as a 25th anniversary of the first event, these gruelling runs demand meticulous car preparation and tremendous self-discipline – but generate fantastic camaraderie between entrants.

Saloon car racing

Back to the glory days, pure and simple, with Anglias, BMW 2000s, Alfa GTAs and Minis scrabbling round on Dunlop racing tyres in scenes straight from the 60s.

Historic single-seater and sportscar racing

From ERA through Maserati 4CM and Alfa Monzas, including Blower Bentleys and Mercedes SSKs, right up to fairly recent Formula 1 material, this evocative, heady mix stirs up memories for everyone. In the sportscar class, glorious packs of Lotus Elevens battle it out with Jaguar D-types, Maseratis, Birdcages and Coopers too. But you have to be rich.

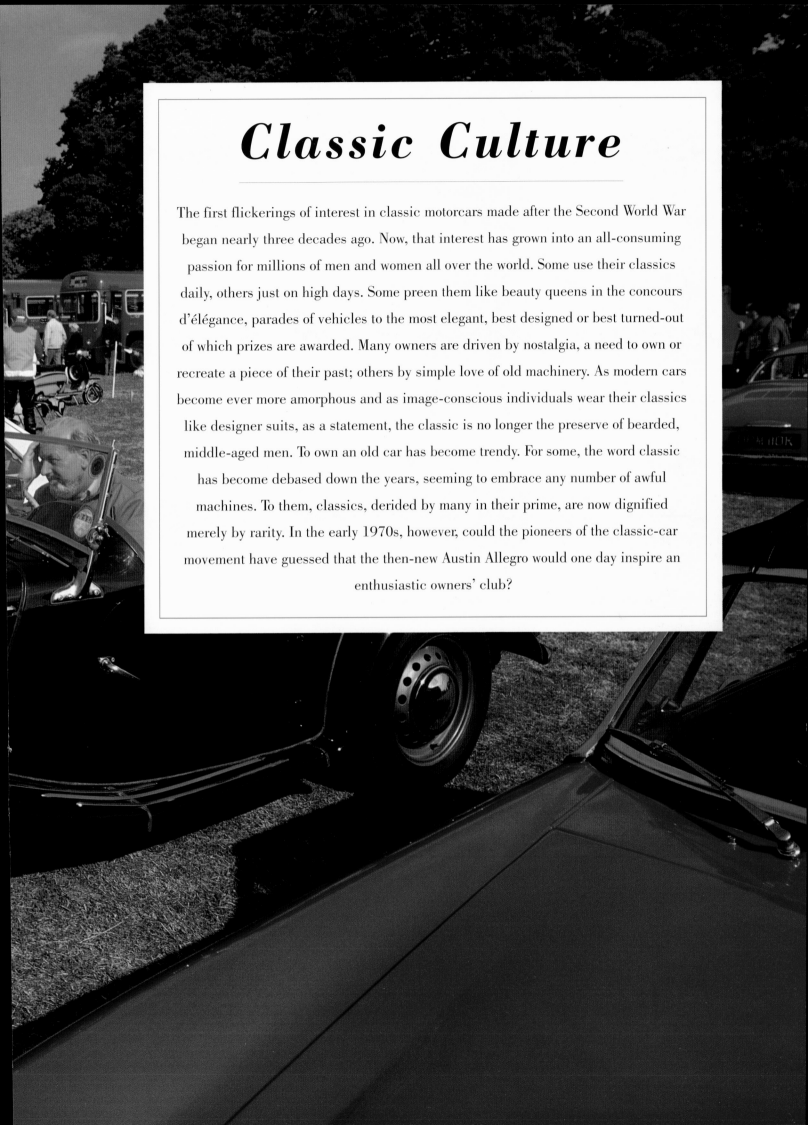

Classic Culture

The first flickerings of interest in classic motorcars made after the Second World War began nearly three decades ago. Now, that interest has grown into an all-consuming passion for millions of men and women all over the world. Some use their classics daily, others just on high days. Some preen them like beauty queens in the concours d'élégance, parades of vehicles to the most elegant, best designed or best turned-out of which prizes are awarded. Many owners are driven by nostalgia, a need to own or recreate a piece of their past; others by simple love of old machinery. As modern cars become ever more amorphous and as image-conscious individuals wear their classics like designer suits, as a statement, the classic is no longer the preserve of bearded, middle-aged men. To own an old car has become trendy. For some, the word classic has become debased down the years, seeming to embrace any number of awful machines. To them, classics, derided by many in their prime, are now dignified merely by rarity. In the early 1970s, however, could the pioneers of the classic-car movement have guessed that the then-new Austin Allegro would one day inspire an enthusiastic owners' club?

WORKING CLASSICS

The attributes that make a vehicle a classic also bring the best cars to the top in the tough world of work. This applies whether services need them to be out in all weathers rescuing stranded motorists, attending a breakdown or accident, pursuing villains and keeping traffic flowing or simply carting goods around reliably.

Each service has its favourites, each vehicle's special abilities suiting it to its chosen job. The Automobile Association (AA) (1905), finding its motorcycle-and-sidecar outfits no longer efficient, bought Land-Rovers almost from inception in 1948 to aid motorists.

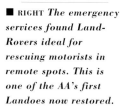

■ RIGHT *The "woody" estate, a popular variation on a saloon car which could carry more.*

■ RIGHT *The emergency services found Land-Rovers ideal for rescuing motorists in remote spots. This is one of the AA's first Landoes now restored.*

■ ABOVE *Rare Aston Martin shooting brakes (estate cars) based on the DB5.*

■ RIGHT *The Ford Thames was available in van and pick-up forms. Designed to drive in a similar way to a car, it was ancestor to the ubiquitous Transit.*

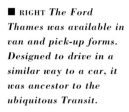

Likewise, the Royal Automobile Club (RAC) (1897) used a selection of cars and car-derived vans: Austin Sevens, Morris Minors and then Mini-vans for lighter-duty breakdowns and Bedford CA vans and trucks at the heavier end before they universally adopted the Ford Transit in the 1970s. In the 50s, the RAC ran six Isetta bubblecars in London to reach motorists through the clogged traffic. These tiny two-strokes' towing ability is not recorded!

Policemen and postmen

The police have long used big, powerful and reliable saloons, from the classic, fast, bell-equipped and evil-handling Wolseleys of the 50s to the Rovers and Jaguars of the 70s. Various forces have at times tried to beat the villains at their own game by adopting the same wheels – Jaguar MkIIs in the 50s and Lotus Cortinas in the 60s. The police have also tried out new types of vehicle. In the 60s, forces ran an experimental four-wheel-drive

■ LEFT *The Citroën "H" van was the backbone of many small businesses in France.*

(by Ferguson Formula) Ford Zodiac Mk4, which may have paved the way for the near-universal adoption of the classic, big-hearted Range Rover for motorway patrols.

In the 50s, a Morris Minor van with ugly rubber wings was a familiar sight. Britain's General Post Office (GPO) thought the wings were unbreakable and immune to minor knocks. Alas, they meant the headlamps sat up in separate pods and setting alignment was nigh-on impossible. The GPO then turned to another car-derived van, the Bedford version of the first Vauxhall Viva, the HA of 1963. In France, the entire postal service was served by a pair of rugged, front-wheel-drive hold-alls, the Citroën 2CV and Renault 4 vans.

Civilian workers

For "civilian" use, car-derived vans have long been another way for makers to sell to motorists unfamiliar with the size and vision difficulties of the large-panel vans like them. Since the 1920s, panelled-in versions of most popular cars have been available. They are often simply an estate version with the windows filled in and the back seat missing. Before Purchase Tax applied to commercial vehicles, this was the cheapest way to own an estate car – buy a van and fit side windows!

Ford's Transit of 1968 was the trendsetter whose name became generic for one-tonne (1,016kg) vans. This much-loved, tough and surprisingly fast hauler was a natural to carry everything from parcels to builders' gear. It was a big hit with criminals, too: they could hide in it until the coast was clear and carry a lot of booty. Where there's work to be done, the chances are you'll find there will be a classic that has completed it.

■ ABOVE *The Ford V-eight Pilot, an attractive and powerful chase car in its day.*

■ BELOW LEFT *Some Dutch police forces used the Porsche 911.*

■ BELOW RIGHT *Many forces in Britain used unusual machines – such as this MU2 Lotus Cortina.*

CLASSICS ON FILM AND TV

Nothing does more for a classic car's kudos than appearing in a classic film or television series. Who could forget the Volvo P1800 in Britain's *The Saint* series of the 60s or the Alfa Spider in *The Graduate* (1967) with Dustin Hoffman? Both made these cars world-famous and boosted sales. As dynamic and often beautiful objects, motorcars have always looked good on screen as set decoration or the focus of the action. The catalogue of classic-car screen moments is huge.

The Americans have long been masters of putting the motorcar on screen, in everything from Herbie *The Love Bug* (1969) to cult films like *Vanishing Point* (1971), *Two-Lane Blacktop* (1971) or *Duel* (1971). For many connoisseurs it is the 1968 film *Bullitt* starring Steve McQueen that features perhaps the best car chase ever filmed: his Mustang pursues a sinister Dodge Charger at speed through the hilly streets of San Francisco to a superb V-eight soundtrack. The scene lasts 12 minutes,

■ LEFT *MkII Jaguars featured as heavily as getaway cars on film as in real life.*

■ BELOW *An S-Type Jaguar appeared in the 1967 film Robbery.*

■ BELOW *A white Volvo P1800 became a trademark for The Saint played by Roger Moore.*

■ LEFT *Big saloons featured in many British crime films: Richard Burton, Jaguar S-Type in Villain (1971).*

with McQueen, a good driver, doing much of the stunt work himself. In his 1971 film *Le Mans*, McQueen did more driving than acting and added to the list of motor-racing films such as *The Green Helmet* and *Grand Prix* (1966) and *Winning* with Paul Newman (1969) that were neither critical nor box-office successes.

■ RIGHT *What the public did not see – Michael Caine providing extra damage to the red E-Type in The Italian Job (1969).*

Cops, robbers and spies

In British films, the crime genre has long been a fertile hunting ground for classic-spotters. *Robbery* (1967, based on the Great Train Robbery) has a hair-raising pursuit with a police S-Type Jaguar and felons in a silver Jaguar MkII. In *The Italian Job* (1969), a tongue-in-cheek take of an audacious gold robbery starring Michael Caine and Noël Coward, cars outshone actors. The getaway cars are three Mini Coopers that make a cheeky escape along Turin rooftops and drains. Other motorized stars include a Lamborghini Miura, a pair of E-Types and an Aston Martin DB4 convertible. Jaguars provide aura in gangland classics like *Performance* and *Get Carter* (both 1971), while *Villain* (1971), starring Richard Burton, features a payroll heist: look out for the Jaguar S-Type, Ford Zodiac and Vanden Plas three-litre, all wrecked. And look out for the Lamborghini Islero and the Rover 3.5 in *The Man Who Haunted Himself*, also of 1970.

James Bond films feature cars heavily as part of 007's equipment. The gadget-laden Aston DB5 caused a sensation when it appeared in *Goldfinger* in 1964 with its ejector seat,

machine guns and radar. Toyota built a special convertible 2000GT for *You Only Live Twice* (1967) but it had no real gadgets. In *On Her Majesty's Secret Service* (1969) new Bond George Lazenby drove a stock Aston DBS and a Mercury Cougar in an ice-racing sequence.

■ ABOVE *A Lotus Elan starred alongside Emma Peel and John Steed in The Avengers.*

■ LEFT *The British TV series, The Sweeney featured Jaguars weekly.*

■ LEFT *Goldfinger: 007's Aston Martin DB5 featured overrider hooks, machine guns behind sidelights and revolving number plates. Three more were built for Goldeneye (1995).*

CHOOSING & OWNING A CLASSIC

Saloon or estate, two doors or four, open or closed – only you know which type of classic will suit your needs and pocket but, generally speaking, options like power steering, overdrive and air conditioning are always worth searching out if you want the most usable classic in modern conditions. Be prepared in most cases for higher maintenance costs or a lot more unreliability than with a modern car.

Bodywork bother

Rust is the biggest enemy of the older car. Before the 1980s most ordinary – and indeed many expensive – motorcars were only given token rust-proofing, so if you live in a damp climate corrosion will be much more of a problem. Unitary or monocoque construction was coming in across the board by the 60s on mass-produced cars, and any rust in the sills, floor or inner wing areas with this type of bodywork will seriously compromise the car's strength and rigidity.

Cars with separate chassis are generally less of a worry because the bodywork is not self-supporting. That doesn't mean the chassis won't rust eventually, and removing bodywork for restoration is not for the faint-hearted. Aluminium panels – as found on high-calibre

classics like Aston Martins – don't rust in the same way but do suffer from electrolytic action between the aluminium and the steel frame of the car. Aluminium is also more susceptible to damage. Glass-fibre bodywork doesn't rust, of course, and in most cases – apart from the Lotus Elite – features a separate steel chassis, too. However, the passage of time can cause the gel coat to craze, which is a specialist job to rectify. Taking paintwork more generally, look for signs of over-spray on door rubbers and window surrounds, indicating a hasty respray. Brightwork – badges, bumpers, grilles, etc – is

■ ABOVE *The Triumph Spitfire is a relatively easy car to restore because of its separate chassis.*

■ BELOW *A bubblecar could be an ideal project for those with limited space.*

■ LEFT *There are still plenty of unrestored "popular" classics to choose from.*

notoriously costly to refurbish and many pieces are difficult to find for more unusual models.

Mechanical matters

Mechanically, older cars tend to be simpler, although by the end of the 60s fuel injection and complex air suspension was putting many of the more expensive cars beyond the abilities of the home mechanic. Generally, with the engine, you should be looking for signs of excessive smoke from the exhaust and of overheating with watercooled engines, particularly if they are of exotic aluminium construction as with many Alfa Romeo and Lancia models. Gearboxes should be reasonably quiet, though many 50s and even 60s cars featured "crash" bottom gears which give a rather evocative whine. Automatic gear changes won't be as smooth as on a modern luxury car but, even so, changes shouldn't be rough, either. Woolly steering and soggy brakes characterize many big saloons of the classic era, but many sportscars of the 50s and 60s have handling that is rewarding.

Looking inside

Although scruffy interior trim won't stop you driving a classic, a car's interior condition is vital to its feel and ambience. A Jaguar, for instance, with damp carpets, peeling wood

■ ABOVE LEFT *The interior of this "woody" station wagon would be complex and expensive to put right.*

■ ABOVE *Welding is a useful skill if you intend to tackle restoration yourself.*

■ ABOVE RIGHT *It is essential that leather and wood are in good condition. Refurbishment is expensive.*

■ BELOW *Rust curses cars of the 1950s and 1960s such as this Jaguar.*

veneer and cracked or split leather seats loses much of its appeal. Retrims are expensive and obscure interior parts difficult to source. The generally far more basic interiors of sportscars are easier to refurbish and, again, for the popular British marques everything is usually available. Hoods are expensive to replace on sportscars – look out for tears – while a hard top is definitely worth paying extra for if you intend using an open classic all year. If you are determined to buy a classic car, do your homework. Join the relevant club, get to know the pitfalls of the model you are after, then go out and look at as many as you can before making a decision.

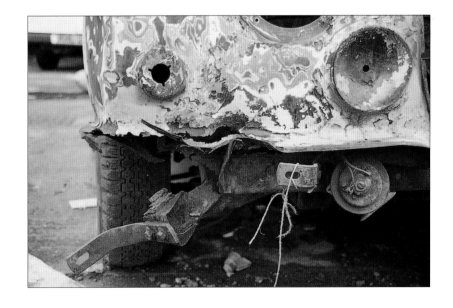

FUTURE CLASSICS

New "classics" appear all the time. These are cars that, because of sheer appeal, excellence or exclusivity, are instantly memorable and desirable from first sightings at a motor show. Others, cult darlings such as the Golf GTI, have become the definitive cars of their era and have never truly fallen out of fashion with enthusiasts. Others again, such as the Mini, VW Beetle or 2CV, still in or recently out of production, are simply the modern versions of

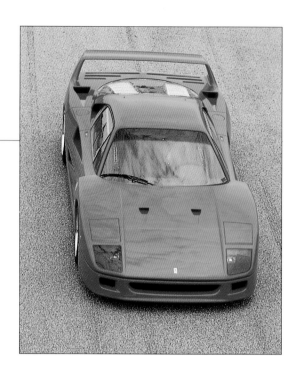

■ RIGHT *All Ferraris will be classics, especially the stunning, 200mph (321kph)-topping supercar F40 of which 1500 were made.*

■ FAR LEFT *Mazda's MX5 aped the Lotus Elan of 20 years earlier – but bits did not fall off.*

■ LEFT *BMW's M3 was a fine-handling supersaloon. Later versions could not quite match its raw appeal.*

acknowledged classic designs. They don't have to be supercars to qualify, although some of the most obvious contenders clearly are: any new Ferrari or Lamborghini is so eagerly awaited that its status upon arrival is guaranteed. In these cases, simply belonging to the right marque is enough to confer immortal desirability.

Porsche 911s all qualify as future classics because of their unique blend of robustnesss and driveability, even if the dashboard design is as confusing as ever. The wide-bottomed 928 will forever hover on the fringes of true classicdom, although some of the early 944 Turbos will be allowed into the hallowed club, and the Speedster-inspired Boxster is clearly on the VIP list from the word go. It's all a question of attitude.

Dodge's awesome eight-litre V-ten Viper has

■ RIGHT *First of the breed – the VW Golf GTi. Purists say the first, lightest cars were the best. This is an 1800cc MkI.*

■ RIGHT *The Delta Integrale was a homologation special built so that Lancia could win rallies. It made a scorching road car, too.*

■ RIGHT *Classic coupé, German style. BMW 635 coupés were fine-handling cruisers.*

■ ABOVE *US brutality. The Dodge Viper with its eight-litre V-ten engine is a "Cobra for the 90s".*

■ BELOW *The Peugeot 205GTI, the classic hot hatch, once described as a Mini Cooper for the 1980s. High insurance premiums killed off this breed of car.*

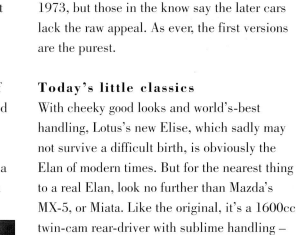

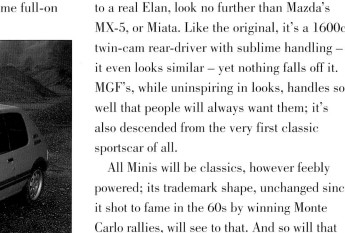

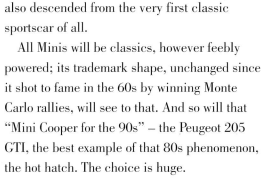

already made a name for itself as the AC Cobra of the 1990s, but its compatriot the Corvette has never been the same since it was emasculated after 1970. Nearly all TVRs occupy the same specialist slot – they are beefy, brutal, British and rear-drive, with that gorgeous V-eight woofle. The Ford Escort RS Cosworth and Sierra Cosworth, both astonishingly fine road cars, have won themselves a place in the hearts of the sort of people who worshipped anything that followed the rally-winning RS Escorts out of Ford's Advanced Vehicle Operation at Boreham, Hertfordshire, in the 1970s. Buying yourself a Lancia Delta Integrale gives the same full-on driving appeal with even more exclusivity. The first-shape BMW M3 of the late 80s falls into much the same bracket – a rock-hard driving machine – and effectively upgrades the reputation carved out by the 2002 Turbo in 1973, but those in the know say the later cars lack the raw appeal. As ever, the first versions are the purest.

Today's little classics

With cheeky good looks and world's-best handling, Lotus's new Elise, which sadly may not survive a difficult birth, is obviously the Elan of modern times. But for the nearest thing to a real Elan, look no further than Mazda's MX-5, or Miata. Like the original, it's a 1600cc twin-cam rear-driver with sublime handling – it even looks similar – yet nothing falls off it. MGF's, while uninspiring in looks, handles so well that people will always want them; it's also descended from the very first classic sportscar of all.

All Minis will be classics, however feebly powered; its trademark shape, unchanged since it shot to fame in the 60s by winning Monte Carlo rallies, will see to that. And so will that "Mini Cooper for the 90s" – the Peugeot 205 GTI, the best example of that 80s phenomenon, the hot hatch. The choice is huge.

INDEX